THE LIBERATION OF SOPHIA

by
David Hayward

ISBN-13: 978-1497524668
ISBN-10: 1497524660

DEDICATION

I want to dedicate this to my wife, Lisa. Some psychologists suggest that a man will discover in the woman he is attracted to the reflection of his anima, his inner female. The mysterious and beautiful feminine that he is blind to in himself he adores in the woman in front of him.

If this is true, then it would follow that Lisa is the external embodiment of my inner Sophia, my feminine side.

She truly is mysterious. She truly is beautiful. She truly is wise.

And it is her wisdom, her sophia, that was very instrumental in helping me survive one of the most difficult, arduous and potentially fatal journeys of my life.

Thank you, Lisa.

ACKNOWLEDGEMENTS

I want to thank my family, my friends, my fans, and my foes. They have all played a part in my story and the development of the story of Sophia.

Interior designed by Greg Knudson, www.gregknudson.com
Cover design by Eric Lawrence, redworksproductions@gmail.com

TABLE OF CONTENTS

Introduction	1	Cleansed	63
Tightrope	3	Crouch	65
Hills	5	Resonance	67
Window	7	Waiting	69
Trapped	9	Surrender	71
Escape	11	Grateful	73
Leap	13	Branching	75
Home	15	Transparent	77
Exposed	17	Canoe	79
Vulnerable	19	Study	81
Hollow	21	Balance	83
Clearing	23	Conquer	85
Blacksheep	25	Fearless	87
Wild	27	Might	89
Pioneer	29	Steadfast	91
Hide	31	Agreement	93
Bridge	33	Shelter	95
Tracks	35	Rooted	97
Defiance	37	Longing	99
Distant	39	Wisdom	101
Solitary	41	Provision	103
Lake	43	Summit	105
Cave	45	Deconstruction	107
Upsidedown	47	Freedom	109
Suspended	49	Release	111
Flow	51	Rising	113
Primal	53	Metamorphosis	115
Entangled	55	Angel	117
Rebel	57	Light	119
Nightmare	59	Conclusion	122
Deep	61		

INTRODUCTION

I left the professional ministry and the church abruptly in the spring of 2010.

I'd finally had enough. I wanted to be free. I needed to be free. What I discovered, though, was that I was free all along. I simply needed to live it.

At the time my wife Lisa was working Friday and Saturday nights. So I had both of those nights to do my artwork in solitude. I have been an artist most of my life, usually focusing on producing moody watercolor landscapes. But suddenly I found myself using pencils and pens. I was drawing these detailed images of a young girl or woman in various situations. She was usually nude and almost always seen from behind, engaging with nature, animals, birds, water, fish, the elements, but always essentially with herself.

One evening, as I was drawing "Cave", I noticed an incredible amount of emotion within me as I drew her. It was then I realized I was drawing my own journey, chronicling my own spiritual passage. I knew her name was Sophia and that she represented the pilgrimage from being trapped to being free. At the same time I noticed how many people, especially women, were intrigued, inspired and encouraged by her as I posted each image on my blog, nakedpastor.

It wasn't even really intentional. It was like a flow of consciousness. I only drew whatever I was inspired to draw whenever I was inspired to draw it. The images kept flowing for over two years until I had collected over fifty-five of them. When I finished the last drawing, I knew I was done. It was finished. Sophia, I, had finally found the freedom longed for.

So when you read the story of Sophia and see the drawings, you are seeing not only the journey of a young woman courageously struggling to achieve her own spiritual independence and gain her own freedom. You are also reading my story. This is about me. But it is also about so many of you who feel or felt trapped and want to do whatever it takes to be free.

Don't make the mistake, like I did, of assuming that liberation from captivity is easy. It's not. It is full of danger. But if you journey it well, you will come into a freedom like you've never known before. You have to adjust to it. I hope this book helps. I think this is why the moon plays a significant role in this story: it is the dark night of the soul. There is very little light, and what light there is, is reflected. But I can say that if you persevere, you will come into a light as bright as the sun… your own light.

I intentionally never show Sophia fully. We never see her face. That's because she is all of us.

Take the journey with me.

TIGHTROPE

The way is narrow. Few find it.

This is a recurring dream:

There is a deep and fast river that I must cross. But it is too dangerous. I find a rope tied between two trees on the opposite banks of the river. I cross over the river on this tightrope. I am being judged by those watching. They are waiting to see if I will fall.

It has come to this.
It seems I am always being watched.
Always being judged.
People are always waiting to see me fall.

The line I must walk is very narrow. Treacherous. If I fall I will perish.

When I was a child I had another recurring dream. I had this dream whenever I was sick with a fever. Like clockwork. This is the dream:

I am in my house. I have a huge massive thing I'm carrying on my shoulders. It reminds me of Atlas with the entire earth on his shoulders. I must carry this downstairs into the basement. There I stand before a line of austere men and women behind a long desk who will judge me. The burden is so huge and I am terrified of failing.

Fierce and afraid. Why do these two things abide within me simultaneously?
How can I be courageous and afraid at the same time?
Is it my courage acting in the face of fear?

Sometimes…

the fear of being watched,
the fear of judgement,
the fear of disappointing people,
the fear of failure,
the fear of being punished…

is so great that it paralyzes me.

But only for a time. Eventually I always manage to find the nerve to get on that tightrope and walk to the other side… my destination.

HILLS

I look out over the hills. Where is my help going to come from?

Me.

I remember when I was a child.

In my captivity, these memories fill my dreams.

They make me wonder where my wonder went.

Why do I see myself alone in the woods?
Why am I all alone standing on the brow of that hill?
Why am I overlooking the vast valleys of wilderness?

Even though there is a sense of risk, I still feel safe and serene in my solitude. Strength courses through my being.
The fresh wind in my hair makes me feel alive and as free as the wind itself.

Often I would wander off alone. Fearless. Free.

Perhaps these dreams of my childhood freedom are beckoning me.
Perhaps they are calling me back to the innocence,
the confidence,
the fearlessness I once had.
Perhaps they are kind messengers calling me back to this freedom.

This must be true: if I dream about these qualities of innocence, confidence and fearlessness, then they must still reside within me. Somewhere. They are still my possessions. They are already mine.

But they have just been buried under years of neglect. They have been cluttered over with distractions. They have become entangled in things that demanded my attention and allegiance.

Right now they are deep within but emerging in my dreams. I must mine them and make them mine again.

All that is separating them from manifesting in my actual life is me opening my eyes. I will awaken and open my eyes.

Wake up!

I will find that hill and stand upon it again, just like that child.

WINDOW

I'm always waiting.

Looking out the window for something to show is my pastime.
Like through a dark glass.

The thing is… I never really know what I'm looking for.

All I know is that I want to experience my freedom.
The freedom that beats in my chest wants to feel the road.

Windows are good.
They let me see outside of my cell.
Outside of my box.
Outside of my boundaries.

But they are not doors. And I'm looking for a door.
I'm looking out the window for the door.

I learned how to appreciate the present. The now. The here. The be here now.
I know this. I know how to do this now.

But I also know how to hope. How to long. How to desire.
I've learned that desire means lack. I can only desire what I do not have.

What a strange concoction! Desire with contentment. Contentment with desire.

Look at me! I look content. But I'm also waiting.
I'm looking for what I'm looking for.

All these years I have been stretched between these two realities.

Some say to me, "Why can't you just settle down?"
Others say to me, "Why have you settled?"

So I look out the window. Because I'm certain that the opportunity will present itself.

And I will shock everyone because then I will act. They will look for me where I'm supposed to be. But I won't be there. I will be gone. Through the door.

I will escape.

TRAPPED

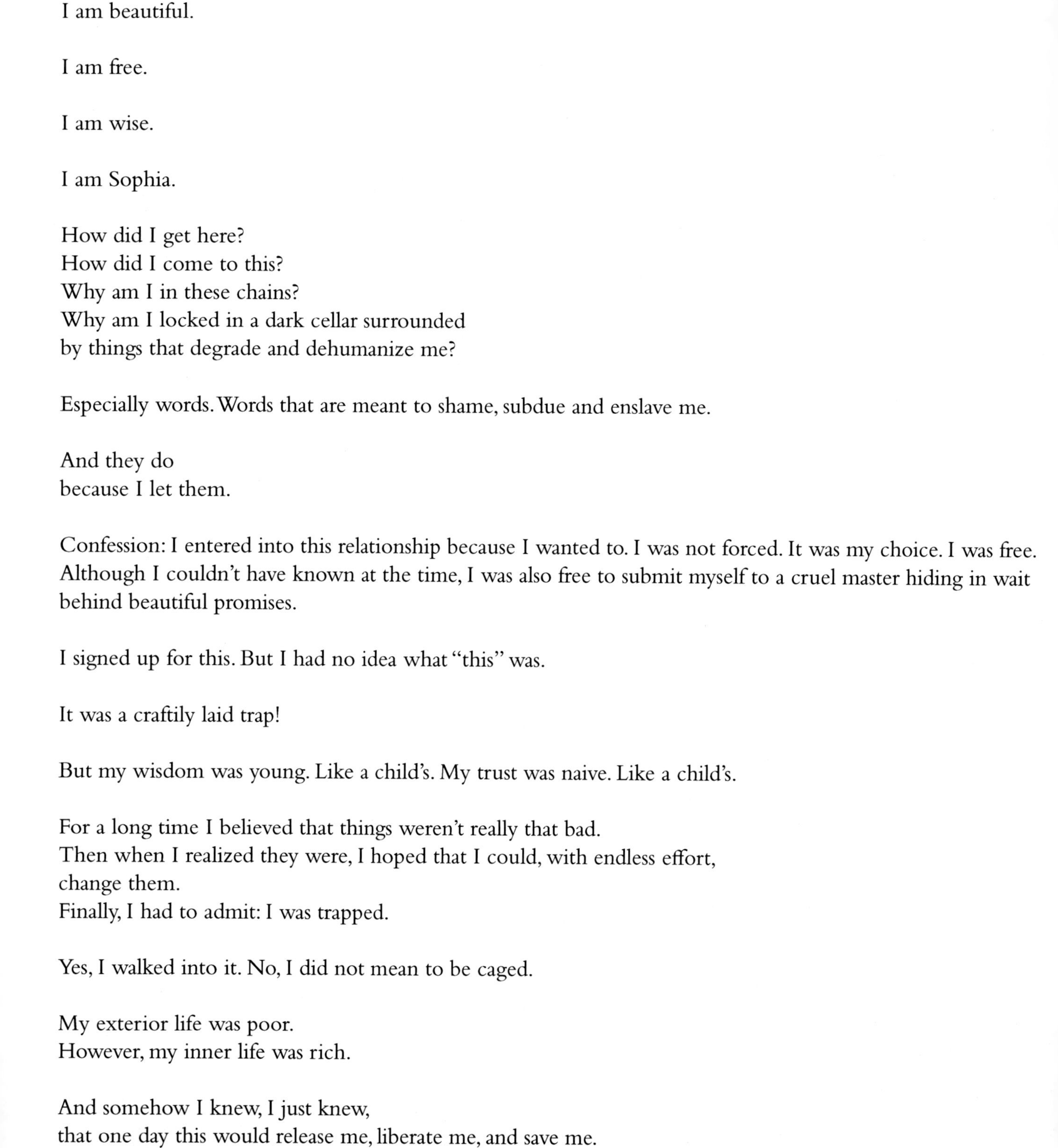

I am beautiful.

I am free.

I am wise.

I am Sophia.

How did I get here?
How did I come to this?
Why am I in these chains?
Why am I locked in a dark cellar surrounded
by things that degrade and dehumanize me?

Especially words. Words that are meant to shame, subdue and enslave me.

And they do
because I let them.

Confession: I entered into this relationship because I wanted to. I was not forced. It was my choice. I was free. Although I couldn't have known at the time, I was also free to submit myself to a cruel master hiding in wait behind beautiful promises.

I signed up for this. But I had no idea what "this" was.

It was a craftily laid trap!

But my wisdom was young. Like a child's. My trust was naive. Like a child's.

For a long time I believed that things weren't really that bad.
Then when I realized they were, I hoped that I could, with endless effort,
change them.
Finally, I had to admit: I was trapped.

Yes, I walked into it. No, I did not mean to be caged.

My exterior life was poor.
However, my inner life was rich.

And somehow I knew, I just knew,
that one day this would release me, liberate me, and save me.
Indeed, I would save myself!

THE WOMAN SHALL
BE SAVED THROUGH
CHILD-BEARING
(1 Tim 2:15)
SUBMIT TO YOUR HUSBAND
(EPHESIANS 5:22)
SEEN AND NOT HEARD
HOME SWEET HOME
A WOMA
PLACE I
IN THE HO
I DO NOT PERMIT A WOMAN TO TEACH.
(1 TIMOTHY 2:12)
WOMAN
DECEIVED.
(1 Timothy 2:14)
DO NOT LET YOUR BEAUTY BE EXTERNAL
(1 PETER 3:3)
CHARITY BEGINS AT HOME
...as the weaker
partner, and
(1 Peter 3:7)

ESCAPE

All it takes is one small opening
and one small opportunity.

Just underneath the straw in my cell I found a hatch door.
My means of escape was always available to me.
I just hadn't seen it yet.

My captors are busy playing their games, planning their next move,
unaware that I have found my means of escape and made mine!

I must make a plan. But I have no idea how to implement it.
All I know is that I must escape.
But I need to be clear how. And when.

I felt like a slave for years. Like I said, I tried to ignore the fact.
Then I tried to change the circumstances.
Finally I had to admit I was enslaved. I had to liberate myself.

But I still needed to know exactly when.
I asked for perfect clarity on when I was to make my decision
and I would act on it immediately.

So many things had to be aligned. Like colossal planets.
Everything had to be perfectly in line. And I knew exactly what had to be in line.

I waited.

Then one day it happened. I knew just as clear as I ever knew anything.
It was time! Immediately. I was done! Done with my slavery.

No time to hesitate. Like the exodus, hastily at night carrying nothing.

So I took a deep breath.
I lifted the hatch door.
And I slipped away.
I stole away as suddenly as a light goes out.
I slipped out of bondage like I slip out of my clothes.

Then I was gone. Never to return.

Escaped.

LEAP

You just have to jump!

Sometimes, like Kierkegaard wrote, you just have to make the leap! I took the existential dare.

What a crazy image this is! Look at me jumping from a great height with only a rope in my hand. How far I must fall! I saw how far it was, and I still made the leap.

Crazy? Or courageous?

Some have asked what the rope is attached to. This you will have to answer for yourself.

For me, it is tied to What Is. I love What Is. What Is rules!

I remember when I made my escape, it was a leap for me. It was full of risk. Full of danger. It was possibly fatal. But I felt death-defying! I could no longer abide my bondage, and the time for me to escape was now.

It is true that I had waited for years for clarity as to when I was to take the leap. To spring my escape. I asked that it would be undoubtedly and unquestionably clear to me when I was to jump. Then, on one cold clear night, the clarity came.

I knew there could be no hesitation.
I knew that calculating was over.
I knew the time was now!

So, just as suddenly as I knew, I leaped!
The most immediate feeling was exhilaration.
Then the next feeling followed fast on its heels, and that was absolute terror.
The leap was irrevocable. There was absolutely no option of going back.
It is finished!

What have I done?
What am I going to do now?
How will I survive this?

But I survived.
I leaped and I landed.
Listen. I am here to tell you about it.

Take the leap. The one you know you must.

HOME

I looked back.

And I didn't turn into a pillar of salt.

I looked back.

When I escaped and I knew I had,
I stopped in my tracks.
It was a night just like this.
The moon was full.
The stars were bright.
The night was cold.
But I was free!
I hadn't felt this feeling in a long time.

The outer freedom finally aligned with my inner one. I was free. Very much alone. Very much afraid. But very much free!

I was suddenly struck with the seriousness of the moment. This was trauma at its finest! This is what crisis looks like! For I was in an in-between place. I was no longer in the place of my captivity. But I hadn't yet found my new home. I was between my cell and my promised land.

I looked back and saw the warmth, the provisions, and the securities of what I'd left. What I'd rejected.

My heart knew, with a huge kind of delicious terror, that I had just launched a terrifying but necessary adventure.

There was no turning back. I was an escapee. I had openly defied my prison. To go back would only make my imprisonment worse. My liberation was public. There was no wishing it never happened. It was done. Irreversibly done!

So here I was in the wide expansive wilderness. It was dark. Only lit by the moon. No direct light. Only reflected. And it was to remain so for a long time. Longer than I expected.
In fact, darkness became my temporary home.

EXPOSED

You will feel exposed.

As I was.

And still am.

Because this is how I choose to live.

When I made my escape it was like ripping myself free from all constraints.
I left all my clothes behind, my given layers of protection.
It left me naked and exposed.

Exposed to the elements.

Even though my freedom dawned within me like the gentle sun rise, when I made it manifest in my outward life it was like throwing open the door to a winter storm,
and it blasted me and everyone around me.

This was my struggle.
Now I know I share this struggle with everyone else who experiences this.
Your inner self demands integration with your outer self.
You can do it by degrees.
But at some point it suddenly becomes evident that you've changed.
For a long time you can hide your transformation.
But eventually it will be exposed.

You will be outed. Either by you or someone else.

You will be exposed.

But this is the comfort it offers: it is you who is exposed,
because your outer shell, your mask,
has finally been ripped away.

You will be laid bare for all to see.

But while my true self was growing within me,
so was my love for it.
So that when I was laid bare for all to see, even though I felt exposed,
I also felt my love for myself come rushing to my defense.
Sure, it was intimidating. True, it was scary. Yes, I was exposed.
But I loved it. And I love it still.

VULNERABLE

From the moment I was aware of my imprisonment I knew I had a choice:
I could become hard-hearted or I could be vulnerable.

I could harden myself in an attempt to avoid further suffering.

Or I could remain vulnerable and enjoy life.

So many vulnerable creatures become victims.

I was determined not to.

I am vulnerable.
But I am not a victim.

What is it about vulnerability that attracts the violent?

Some want to take advantage of it and steal from it.
Like this small baby seal.
It is completely vulnerable and helpless.
So the violent would come and take what is valuable from it.

Others just despise vulnerability. They are repulsed by it and so want to hurt it. They disdain vulnerability and therefore treat it with disdain. They fall upon it because they can't stand weakness either because they are confused by it, frightened by it, or threatened by it.

To learn how to be vulnerable is going to be a lifelong challenge for me. But I do not want to do the opposite and get hard-hearted and fearful. I know my life has been hard. I know I've been mistreated. I know I've been victimized.

But I don't want to make life hard for someone.
I don't want to mistreat others.
I do not want to victimize the vulnerable.

Sometimes I picture myself at the end of my life. Perhaps even on my deathbed surrounded by family and friends. I imagine myself with my heart completely free of resentment where not one grudge remains. I imagine myself extending my love and forgiveness to every person who ever was and is in my life, and receiving the same from them. If they wish.

But whether or not they extend their love to me, it will not change my heart's resolve to love them and accept them and include them in my story.

This is how I picture being vulnerable. That's powerful!

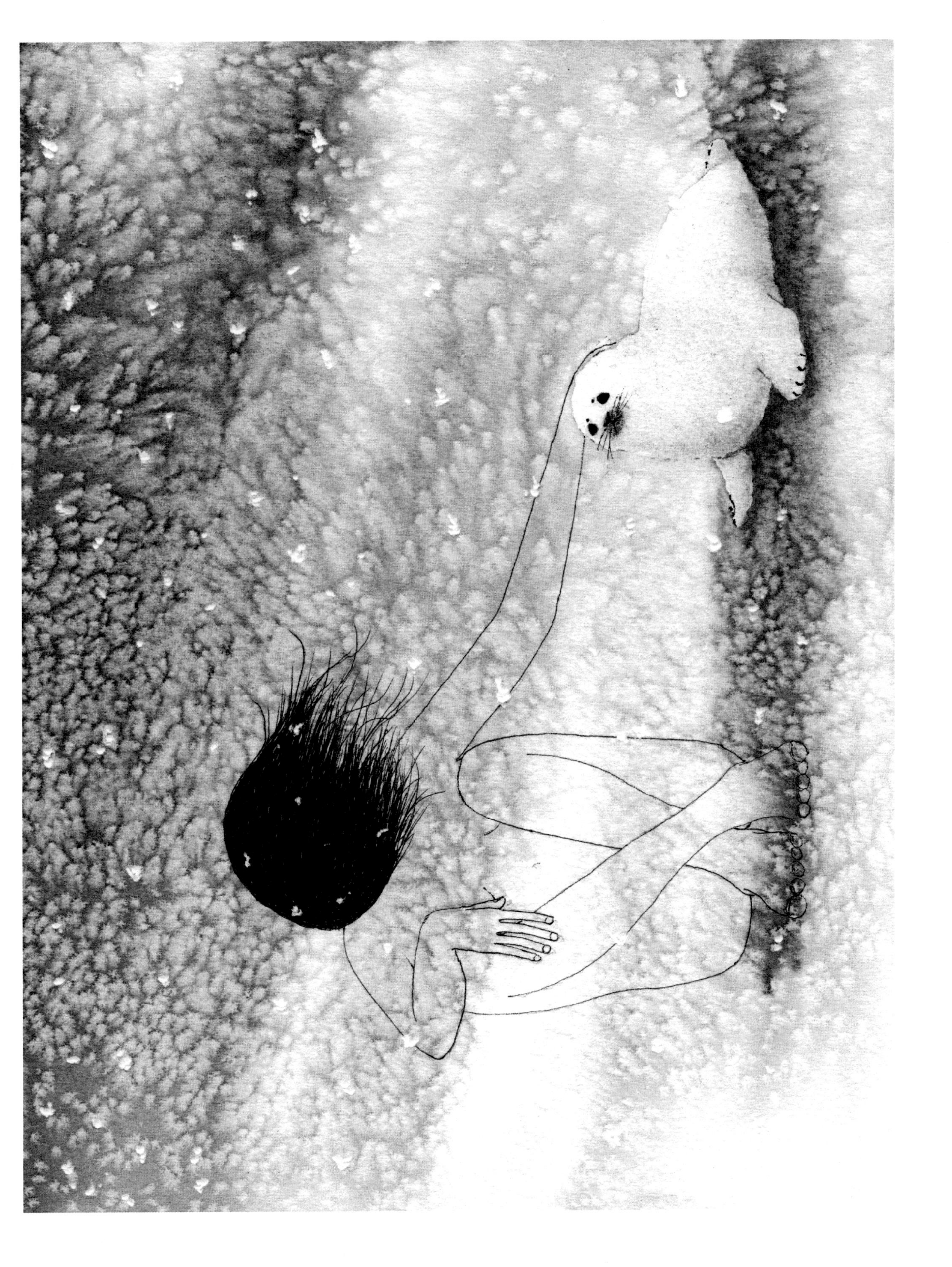

HOLLOW

Hollow.
That's a season.
A season that comes and goes.

When you break free you lose things.
Captivity comes with benefits.

You will miss them. You will want to go back. But don't! Don't be the one who wants to return to the security of the familiar cell. You will be tempted to. But don't!

It is like I got emptied. Reamed out. Scraped clean. Hollowed.
And there was nothing yet to replace it.

When I first broke free from my bondage, I felt numb. In hindsight, I know I didn't really feel anything at the time. I thought I felt free. That was just the external stimuli. I felt it on the outside. It had yet to sink in.

I felt hollow inside. And everything felt hollow outside. Empty.

When I was in my captivity there were people. There was food. There was shelter. There was busy-ness. There was a schedule. There were rituals. There were traditions. There was predictability, security and fulfilled expectations.

I had a destiny. Everyone reminded me of it.

When I escaped, I not only gave up my bonds, but all the benefits that came with them.

I felt hollow.

I sensed a promise that when I gave up all these things that they would be returned to me a hundred-fold. But the hollow between the promise and its fulfillment is dark and empty.

Deep within the hollow I realized that because I gave up all my benefits from the hands of my masters, I would have to learn to provide for myself. I would have to trust that the hollow would be filled again with good things. Not necessarily from the hands of men.

Good things without strings.

Until they came, though, I learned to appreciate this hollowness
and hid myself within it until my provision came.

CLEARING

I didn't want to come out.
I felt safer in the tangled forest of my approved life.
There I could hide in the shadows.
In fact, I was a shadow of what I was to become.

I would be hidden in all the distractions
that made themselves available to me.

I was an expert in camouflage.

I knew how to hide.
Concealing myself had become a talent.

But look at the beauty of the clearing! The bright moon shines from above and illuminates the field.
Everything is clear and clean. No longer closed and cluttered.

Everything within me wanted to step out into the clearing. It beckoned me. The beauty of the clearing called to me.

Come out. Come out. Shine with me.

It wasn't to be noticed.
It wasn't to be seen.
It was to be me.
It was to come clean.

I felt pushed by no one. There were no external pressures applied. In fact, the pressure was to stay put. It was all me. A deep hunger to come out and reveal myself. For me, and for me alone.

In fact, I recognized the dangers involved. The forest is a good place to hide from threats. Coming out into the clearing exposes you to everyone and everything.

You become easy prey.

To come out takes a certain kind of carelessness.
I don't mean the reckless kind.
I mean the kind that would care less what others think.
The kind that calculates the risk and takes it.
The kind that willingly comes clean.
For myself to see, first.
For others to see, second.
If they can and are willing.
The clearing called me. It calls you.

BLACKSHEEP

I strut through the field under the moon as if I own the place.

Because I do! The world is mine. All things are mine.

Black sheep. That's me.

I was always different.

And I always knew it.

But I had a remarkable skill of being able to blend in.

I knew how to conform.
I knew how to comply.
I knew how to keep the peace.
I knew how to maintain the status quo.

For years I did this. It took diligent effort to conceal my truest self. Everyone thought I was one of them. But the whole time I knew I wasn't. My true colors were yet to show.

I was a black sheep in white sheep's clothing. I was a secret.

When the day came, I once and for all shed the pure white cover and revealed my dark side.

The black sheep came forth with a fury!

Isn't it strange though...the relationship between being fiercely different and being just as fiercely rejected? The more unique I become the less welcome I become. The more myself I am the less a part of the flock I am. The more I am me the less I feel like I belong.

My self-confidence increased. So did my enemies. My sense of my own value, increased. So did my critics. My sense of self-acceptance increased. So did my rejecters.

Each and every rejection came as a painful surprise. But the dynamic never surprised me. I knew this is what happens. I knew I would lose people. We don't expect to lose friends or family.

These are painful but necessary realities I've come to accept, embrace and even welcome.

I am blacksheep.

WILD

While I was in captivity I was secretly aware of a wildness within me.
I wouldn't dare share it.

Of course it was mostly theory without practice. At this point.

I dreamed of it.
I hid it.
I sheltered it.
I nursed it.

Others couldn't see it. If they did I would have been corrected. Or it would have been exorcised.

So I hid my wildness like a wolf hides in the wide open.

Camouflaged by my domesticity.

I heard the wolves in my sleep. Like long threads their howls stretched across the moonlit night and laced themselves around my heart. It was only a matter of time when they would pull me with them into the wild.

I've heard it said that you can take a wolf out of the wild
but you can never take the wild out of the wolf.

This is me. No matter how domestic I behave, I am wild like a wolf! You cannot take this from me.

It was a kind of revelation to discover that it doesn't matter how large my heart is. It had been so trained and tamed over the years that it felt too small to contain the wilderness I dreamed of. My heart had become constricted under the pressure of conformity to life's demands and the expectations of others.

But the truth is that my heart is a portal.
It's a door into the expansive wilderness that awaits me.
It's size doesn't matter.

All I had to do was walk through it.

To the dismay of those who witnessed it.

I ran with the wolves.

PIONEER

I am a pioneer. I separated myself from the mainstream. I left the forest with its community of trees. I must navigate my own spiritual path, blaze my own trail and find my own spiritual home.

It's been a while since I escaped. I've been through many traumatic experiences and several small rebellions during my captivity that left me outside of the majority with a firm desire never to return. I don't know how many times I said, "Never again!" For the past little while I've felt like a bad person because of it. A sad and bitter child. A disappointment. I've felt like my "never again"s have been a weakness. A sign of defeat.

One day a different perspective on my story revealed itself to me. I realized that after each traumatic separation from my captors, I have taken some time to recover, maybe years, but then I get back in the game. But my return to the game has always been further away from center. Every time I was back in captivity my captors knew I was even more unbreakable. I would never submit to their control. I was becoming increasingly dangerous.

Perhaps these deaths have actually been births. Perhaps my place is far outside the norm. Perhaps because of fear or insecurity or a desire to please, I would never go far voluntarily, so I had to be coaxed by these small deaths and births to arrive where I am now. A pioneer.

All our heroes, at some point, broke away from the norm, the crowd, the established, to become pioneers, to find their own spiritual property, build their own spiritual homes, to become caretakers of their own lives. Sovereign.

Others are happy just going along with the flow, upholding the status quo and maintaining institutions. They are happy to live and die in the arms of their inherited beliefs and behaviors. They are a stable blessing to the world. But not those who have a sense of adventure and harbor within their breast the urgent necessity to expand their territory and find new ones!

It has always been dangerous and lonely. It is fraught with threats to life and limb. But this fades in importance to the promise of new life, freedom and independence. We will always leave the comforts of home to find new life. There are no maps. The hostiles have not been subdued. We are on our own.

But we can read the stories of those who have done the same thing. They have excellent advice. They have wise warnings. They have useful strategies. These will generally help us on our specific journeys. Like Sophia, I'm going to be a pioneer. I'll do it alone if I must. But I'd love some company.

Who's with me?

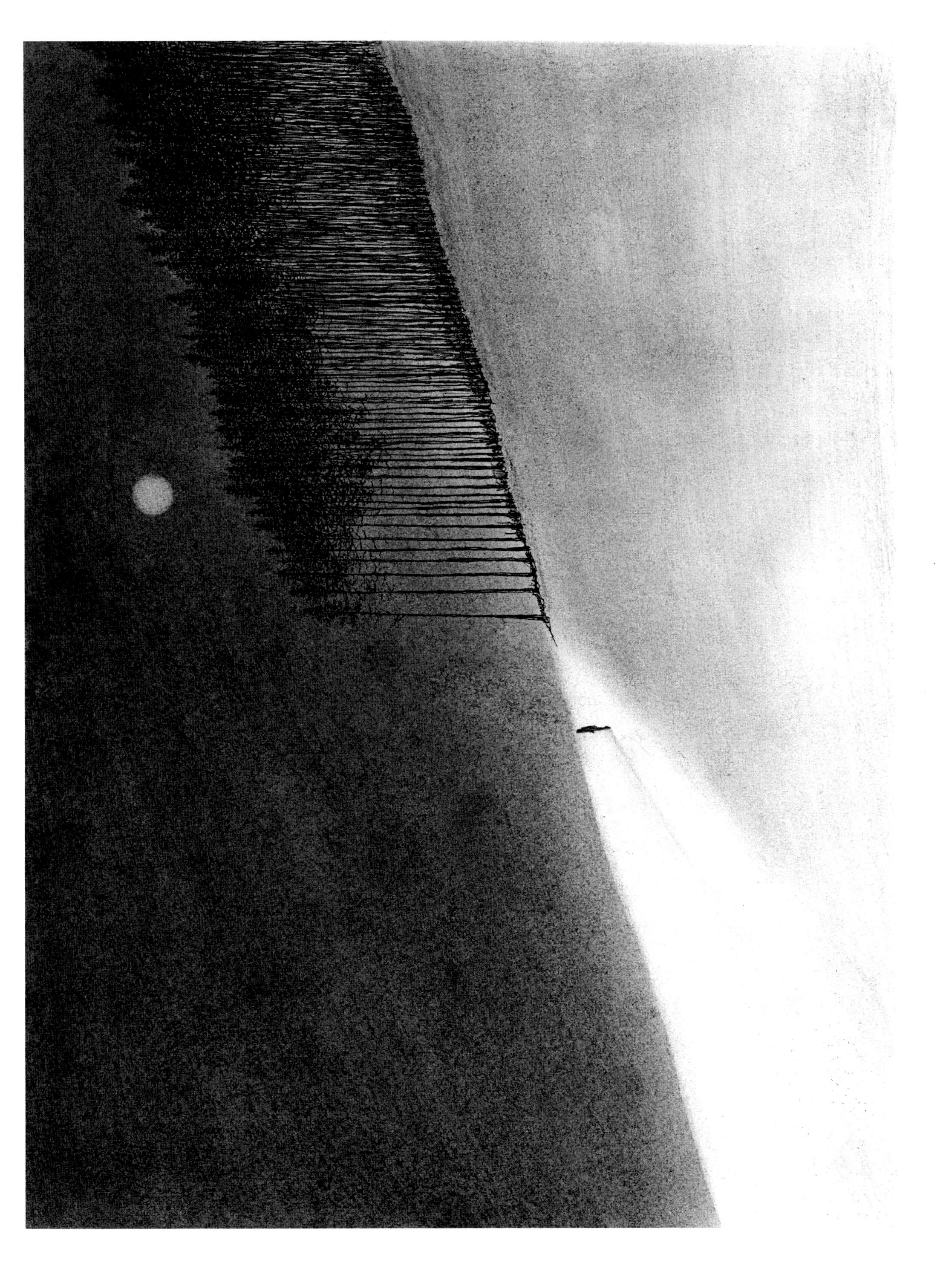

HIDE

It's okay to hide.

I did.

Let me tell you why:
Too many people wanted to find me and restore me to the me I was.
To the me they think I am
and should be.

I couldn't let them do that. No!

So I hid.
I hid myself deep within myself,
far away from their pitiful eyes.

I loved my newfound freedom. I cherished it. It was my treasure, so I buried it in a field and then I bought the field. It was mine and I would never again surrender it.

I could see them coming.
My new freedom gave me new vision.
I have the eyes of an eagle.

Away from their clingy grasps I walked, I ran, I flew!

I wouldn't let them find me.
For to find me was to possess me.

A hole remained where I had been and they wanted me to fill it again.
But I had changed my shape and I would never fit back into their place for me.
I no longer belonged there.

Their constant questions about what I was doing or how I was doing… I couldn't handle them anymore. I couldn't even understand myself. How could I explain myself to them? I was a mystery to myself so an enigma to them.

So I hid.

I could feel them trying to shame me that I had escaped. The temptation to feel guilty about hiding was strong. It never gave up. But neither did I. Deep within I knew that hiding was absolutely necessary for my own health and critical to the security of my freedom.

I hid. Deep in the wilderness and in a high place.

BRIDGE

This was one of the most difficult things I'd ever done.

Burning that bridge. Cutting it down. Separating myself as if permanently.

This didn't necessarily mean forever. But I had to act as if it was. Like an axe!

Look at all those people on the other side. All those faces.
Those are the faces of people I know. People I've loved.

In their own ways, they cared for me.

But I couldn't let them keep me any more.

I had to peel off the desperate fingers of all their expectations.

It was one of the most difficult things I'd ever done.
Their expectations offended me, so I cut them off.
And I did it swiftly.

Apparently it wasn't enough to escape. I had to stay escaped. It is one thing to gain new ground, but it is another to keep it. I'd escaped to new ground. But to keep it I had to secure my liberation from all the noble hopes everyone else held for me. It was time to find, form and fulfill my own.

I've also heard it said that when we leave those we love, we may unconsciously create a crisis in order to justify our departure. Rather than directly betraying them, we develop a scene that makes our leaving inevitable and necessary.

When I escaped their grasp, I created that crisis.
When I cut down all the bridges between us, that sealed the deal.

I had to. I had slipped in and out before. This time I knew it had to be decisive. Final. I really had to leave as if for good. It was abrupt! I know this.

What will happen in the future? I don't know. I don't even want to speculate. Because I have to find myself first. Without a goal. Without a preconceived idea. I just need to know, experience, taste and integrate my freedom.

Who knows?

Bridges can be destroyed.

They can also be built.

TRACKS

Few people want to follow where I go.

I remember reading about a Canadian explorer, David Thompson. The further he travelled into the wilderness the less men would accompany him. He would begin with an entire team with lots of food and gear, but end up with just himself and a few other men with meager supplies.

It is true spiritually as well. The further you wander from civilization, from the norm, from the popular, from the tried and true, the more difficult it is for people to remain with you. You might be up for the exploration and discovery, but they're not!

The fact is that you are on your journey to discover truth because you are passionate about it. Those who accompany you are there to support you. But eventually your passion will outrun their support. Unless they are passionate about discovering the truth too, they will not go all the way with you.

It is a treacherous path the wilderness offers. That's why few go there. That's why it's called the wilderness. I understand the dangers. I know about the risks.

Thomas Merton, a Benedictine monk, applied for years to become a hermit at the Gethsemane Monastery in Kentucky. Some might argue about the conflicts between him and his Abbot, and that his Abbot may have continually blocked his application for less than honorable reasons. But the truth is not just any monk can become a hermit. There are tests one has to pass to be allowed to live alone and be solely responsible for one's own spirituality. It can be spiritually dangerous and even fatal.

Even at times when I felt lost, I wondered if anyone cared. I wondered if anyone would bother to try to find me. I wondered if anyone would track me and rescue me and bring me back. But at the same time I wasn't surprised no one came. It's too dangerous and people know it. I don't blame them.

No wonder few would come with me. No wonder few would care to trace my steps.

People make the mistake of equating freedom with anything goes. They think because I've cast off restraint that I've lost control. In fact it's the contrary. I know how dangerous it is out here. One careless move would bring everything to a halt.

So I have to be more intelligent, more focused, more intentional, more alert, more cautious. I've learned that the most free are the most responsible.

So I will get to where I'm going, for I am where I am.

DEFIANCE

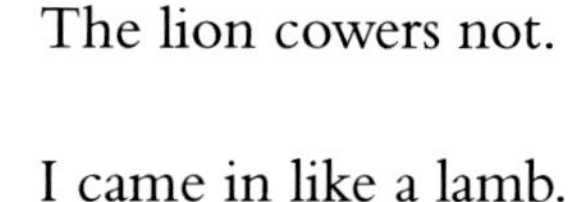

The lion cowers not.

I came in like a lamb.

I will go out like a lion.

For so many years I complied.
For so long I restrained myself under the constraints
of the expectations and demands of others.

In order to keep their peace I kept my tongue.

This, I was told,
this, I was taught,
this, I believed,
this, I practiced,
this was the way a good person should be.
Meek. Mild. Malleable.

I can be these things. I proved it over all the years of my life.

I know how to be meek.
I know how to be mild.
I know how to be malleable.

I am one of the most obedient people I know.

Not that these qualities I became an expert in shall fade away, but they shall certainly fade into their proper place. For something else has been born in me.

Finally! It came late but not too late.
My defiance rose like a hungry lion from its den.

Perhaps my captivity was like a pressure cooker where I was training my hands for war. Perhaps my captivity was the birthing room of my rebellion. This is where my defiance was born!

I will be silenced no more.
Contained no more.
Kept no more.

I will not turn back. I defy all those who would make me.
I will not be devoured again. I won't allow it.

DISTANT

Sometimes I process things by talking about it.
Or writing.
Articulating it helps me know what it is.
Words smith what I'm thinking into shape.

One of my most common coping mechanisms is to go distant.

Ever since I was a child I remember being told that. "You're distant!"
Meaning I'm far away. I've wandered off. Not present.

I just get very quiet and very far away
without moving an inch.

It's a place of silence and solitude. I brood.
If I was alone nobody would say anything.
No one would draw attention to it.
It wouldn't be inappropriate.

But the fact that this happens when I'm with people
makes it noticeable and, for some, sometimes wrong.

There are times when I need to be alone when I'm not and can't.

So I get distant. I wander off in my mind. I retreat within.

What do I think about?
Anything and everything. But mostly it has to do with deep and perplexing ideas and thoughts that require my attention.

You may get this a lot. It's not daydreaming. It's more like day-thinking. People might express concern for you. Others might believe you are in shock. Still others might think you're just being rude. But being distant is a part of this territory.

"I'm sorry, I was somewhere else."
That usually takes care of it.
Or if someone asks, "What are you thinking about?"
I say something like, "The meaning of life."

The fact is I often am. And they're never sure if I'm serious or joking.
But it doesn't matter because these thoughts are mine, they are important to me, and I need to figure things out even if I'm with others at the time.
So sometimes I am distant.

SOLITARY

I abandoned everyone.
I therefore felt abandoned.
Because I was.

I became solitary. Like a hermit.

Solitude is lonely. It's supposed to be. But sometimes the loneliness is felt so severely like a cold fog seeping into the marrow of your bones.

But solitude and loneliness are not the same thing.

Solitude is being alone.
Loneliness is feeling alone.

I know loneliness. It is my breath.

I know solitude. It is my lungs.

There is something very foreboding about this solitude, something at once scary and serene. It is both threatening and promising at the same time.

Like any wilderness.
Like any desert.

When you are in this solitude I know you will feel it.
You will feel like you are on an adventure, but a dangerous one.
You will be fully aware of its risks.

Yes, solitude threatens both life and death.
Because this is where we meet wild animals and demons.
This is where we meet our fiercest temptations.

But I learned to trust it. For it is in this solitude, this wilderness,
where I become most myself. All by myself. Alone. Me.

And I become one with the universe.

I breathed in all of it… I took it all in… the All of it…
and the All became me and I became it.
So I sat on this solitary swing, and the solitude embraced my loneliness,
and consoled it.

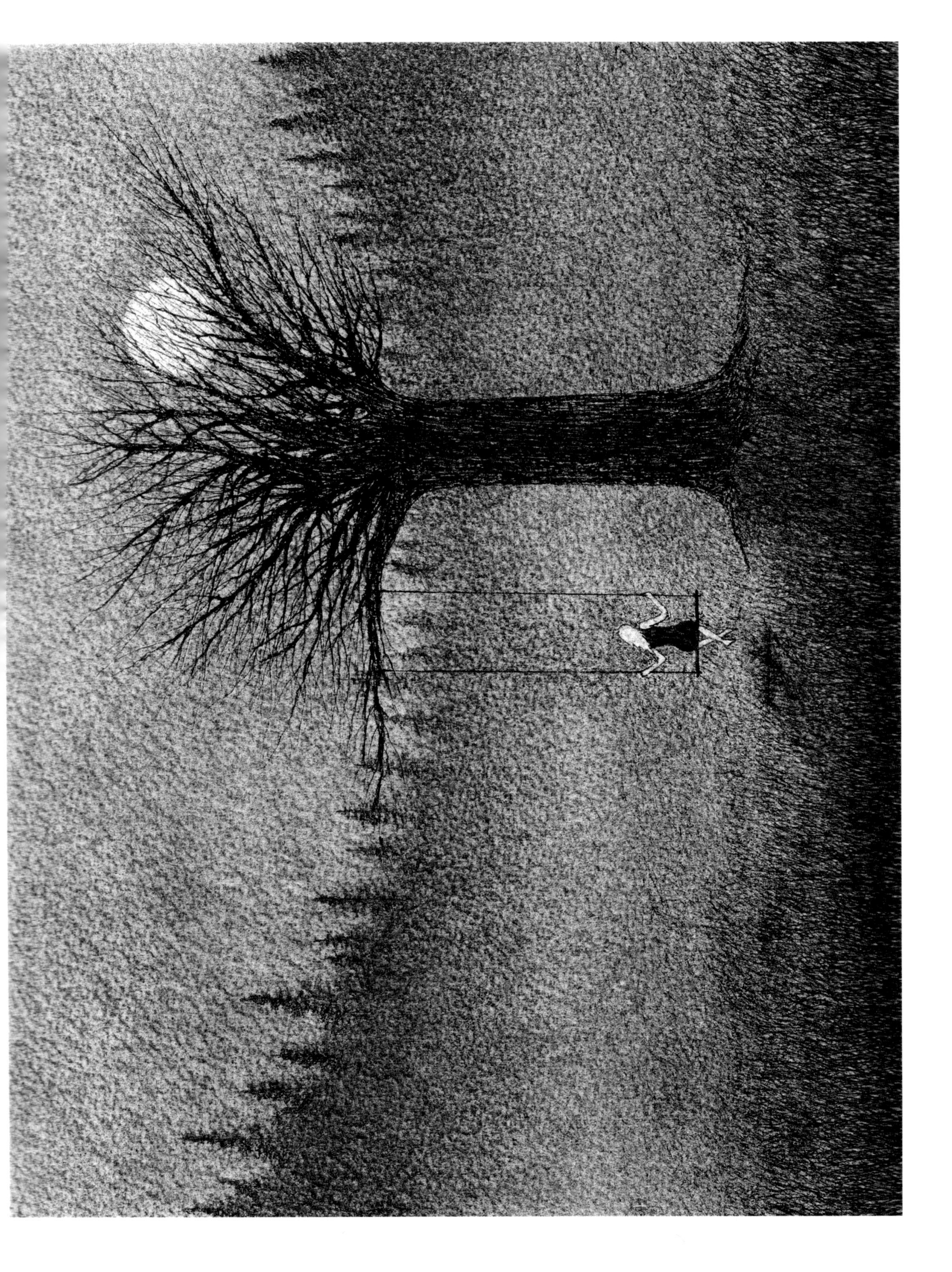

LAKE

Deeper.

Ever since I was a small child I've been terrified of deep water.

What lurks beneath?

But that's where I had to go.

When I escaped,
when I left everything I knew,
when I left my meager comforts,
I foreknew that I was casting myself into the deep.

I was like a boat untied from the dock,
floating away from the safety of the harbor,
and into the fathomless deep.

Nothing could have prepared me for it.
That's why it's so frightening.
It is a darkness into which eyes cannot see.

I look across the lake. It is a cloudy but moonlit night. I see a home on the other side. Smoke rising from the chimney. Its light reflecting on the water.

I want to cross. I need to cross.

Now I'm alone.
There is no one around me.
No one to help.
No one to understand.
No one to even care.

I'm truly alone. I've never really known this feeling of loneliness before. This is an isolation I've never tasted. The truth is I've been reluctant to be responsible for myself. Now it is time.

So rather than extending myself outward to others, I'm being forced to extend myself inward to myself. My deepest self.

I have to go deeper. But I'm scared. I'm afraid of what I will encounter. I will meet the content of my nightmares. Of this I am certain. I must dive into my deepest fears.

But I've committed myself. I will take the plunge.

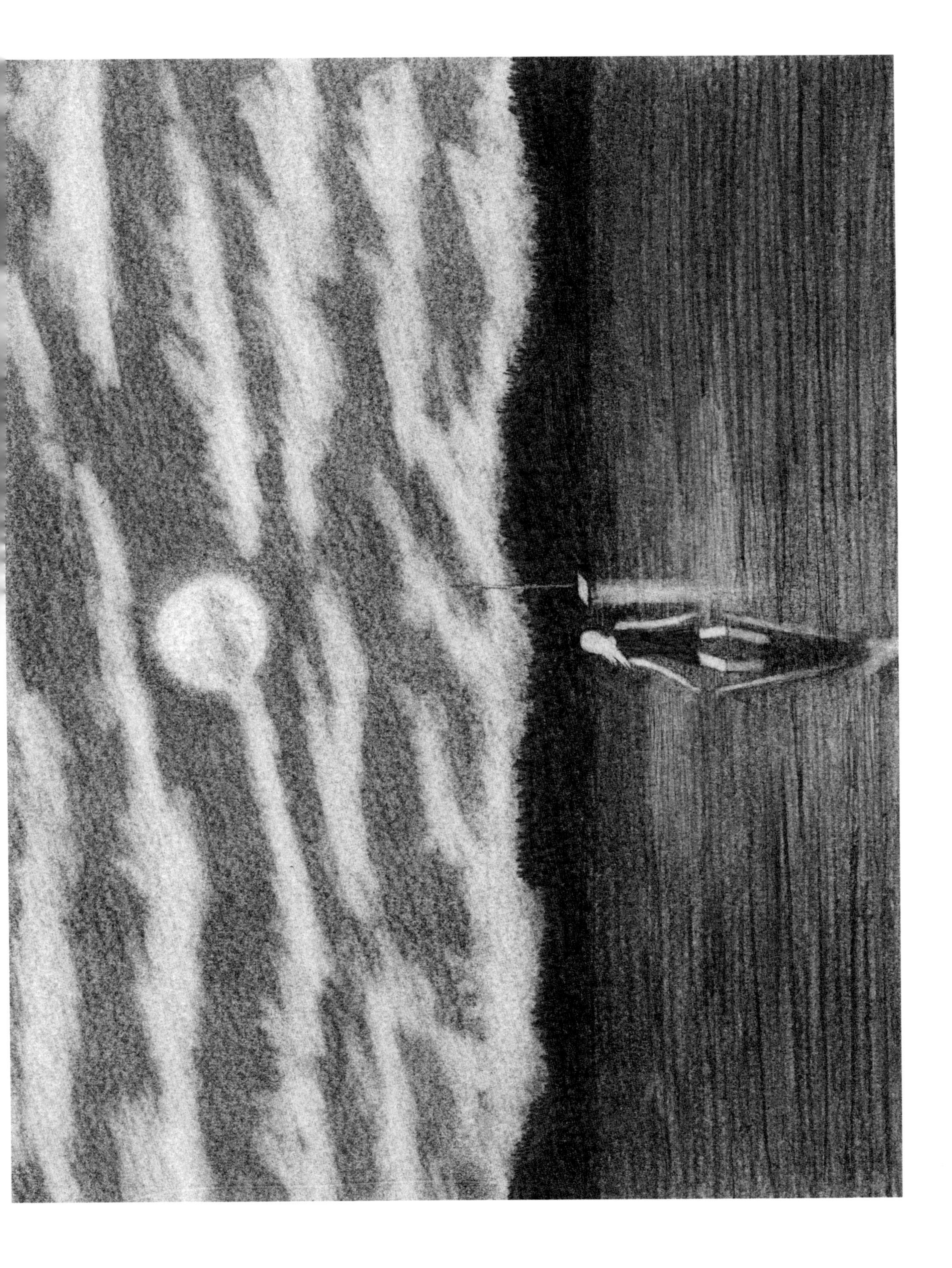

CAVE

I had to make a conscious decision to go deeper.
Deep into a dark place. My inner being. My unconscious.

Fear gripped my heart and wouldn't let it go.

Caves hide creepy things that crawl,
criminals,
ghosts,
skeletons,
beasts
and devils.

There is no natural light.

Whoever goes into a cave comes out
different,
changed,
crazy,
or wise.

But you'll never know unless you go in.
You eventually have to go into your cave.

My unconscious self was fathomless. It still is. Like yours! In fact, it is even more fathomless. The more you discover about yourself the more you discover there is to be discovered. Like an iceberg, your conscious self is like ten percent and your unconscious is ninety. And this never changes.

This is what makes great souls.
I want to be a great soul.

I stood before the entrance of the cave for a long time. I bargained with myself. I argued with myself. I tried to talk myself out of it. Then I dared myself. I never turn down a dare. I finally concluded it was safer to go in than stay out.

A wise man once said you must walk your path or be dragged. So I dragged myself into the cave. I went in.

I emerged different.
I emerged changed.
Some thought I emerged crazy.
But I emerged wise.

My cave was where I was born again.

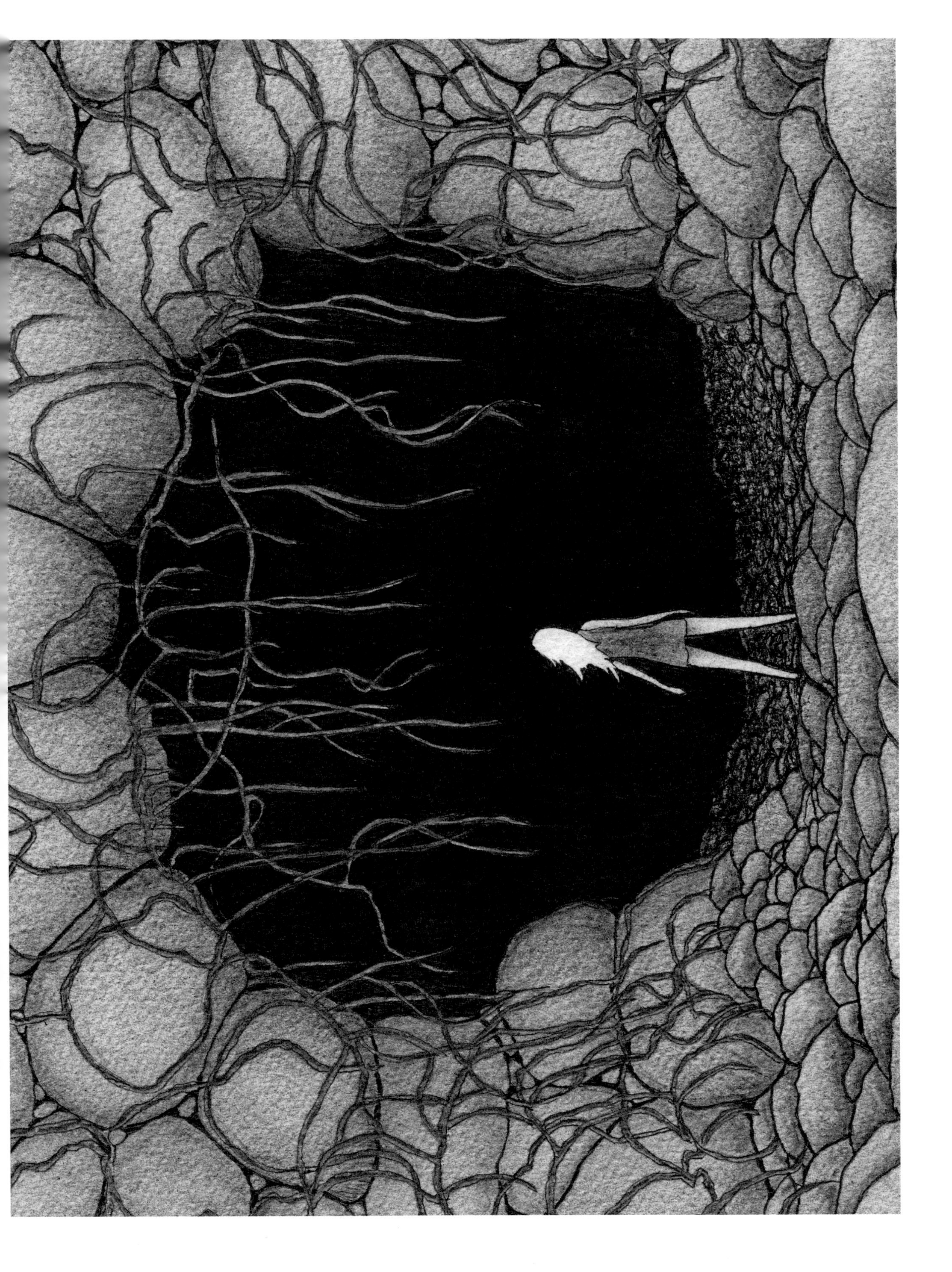

UPSIDEDOWN

My world got turned upside down.

Actually, it was I who got turned upside down.

One day everything is as it is. Then, suddenly, after you make a momentous decision, everything is no longer as it was. Everything changes. Everything! Nothing remains the same. New creations!

It is wisdom to know this. It is like the river into which I step my foot. It is not the same river it was just a moment ago. Neither is it the same river it will be soon. It changes. Even though it is still the river, it has changed. Nothing remains the same.

Nothing is permanent. All is impermanent.

This is what it means to see the world upside down.

I cannot describe how unsettling this is.
Not only do you feel like you are walking in darkness,
but you are completely topsy-turvy.

Disoriented!

I've heard that if you are fitted with glasses that turn everything upside down, eventually your eyes and brain cooperate to make the adjustment and within days they will turn everything right-side up?

So prepare yourself for this.
You're not going crazy.
You're not lost.
You're not in the wrong place.

You're just disoriented.

It takes time to regain your composure. Just like those glasses. Eventually, what you see and don't understand will clarify and make sense.

Sometimes traumatic change means traumatic disorientation.

Don't worry. Give it time. Just wait.
Your eyes and mind will adjust.
You will see clearly again.

SUSPENDED

Here I am suspended between two trees... one dead and one alive.
At times I didn't know whether I was dead or alive.

I was suspended somewhere between them.

Suspended between death and life.

Somehow I knew I wasn't fully conscious. Yet.

Somehow I knew I wasn't fully unconscious. Anymore.

Like sleep.

The problem with being suspended is that it is full of suspense. Day after day after day I lived in a kind of stupor. I felt like I could sleep forever. Exhausted! Fatigued. I knew the acute intensity of my journey was the main contributing factor. I knew I had to move on but I had no strength to do it. I wasn't dead. But I wasn't alive either.

It was my three days in the tomb.
Or thirty.
Or three-hundred.

What do you do in the in-between places?
What do you do between life and death?
What do you do… in a tomb?

Rest. Wait. Sleep.

I was no longer a captive. But I had not yet fully grown into my freedom. I didn't know how to do it. I didn't know how to do freedom.

But I knew it would come. I knew that this long, groggy period of suspension would eventually end.

I knew the stone would be rolled away. I knew the grave clothes would be unwrapped. I knew I would be fully alive. Finally!

But I had to rest. I had to wait. Intentionally.

So I decided to grant myself the fatigue. I made myself rest. I made myself wait.

I was full of suspense.
But I knew I would be full of surprise.
Soon.

FLOW

Not only did I go deep, but in doing so I went against the flow.

Oh my! I do remember joining the "go against the flow" group. We wore it on our t-shirts! But now I'm going against the go-against-the-flow group.

I'm all alone this time.

There were times in my life that I went against the flow simply out of rebellion.

Not this time.

This time it was caused by me desiring more than anything to be true to myself.
To be true to myself I have to know myself.

This was my work.

I never asked to be stared at.
I never planned on becoming a spectacle.
I never desired to be an anomaly.
An enigma.
A riddle.
But that's what I had become to others.

Well, to be fair, I'd become that to myself.
I'm the first to admit I don't understand myself.
So why should I expect others to?

Here's the thing:
people saw what I was.
Then I changed.
That always draws attention.
Not always the best kind.

They were okay with who I was.
They weren't okay who I'd become.

I'm honestly sad to say I can't help that. Because I love them. I care for them. I actually miss them. They don't miss me. They miss who I was.

But this is the kind of journey one must always take alone. I come up for air occasionally, only to be taken even deeper on the next dive. My capacity for depth is increasing. Going deep and against the flow is what I do. I might be alone for now, but at least I'm free forever.

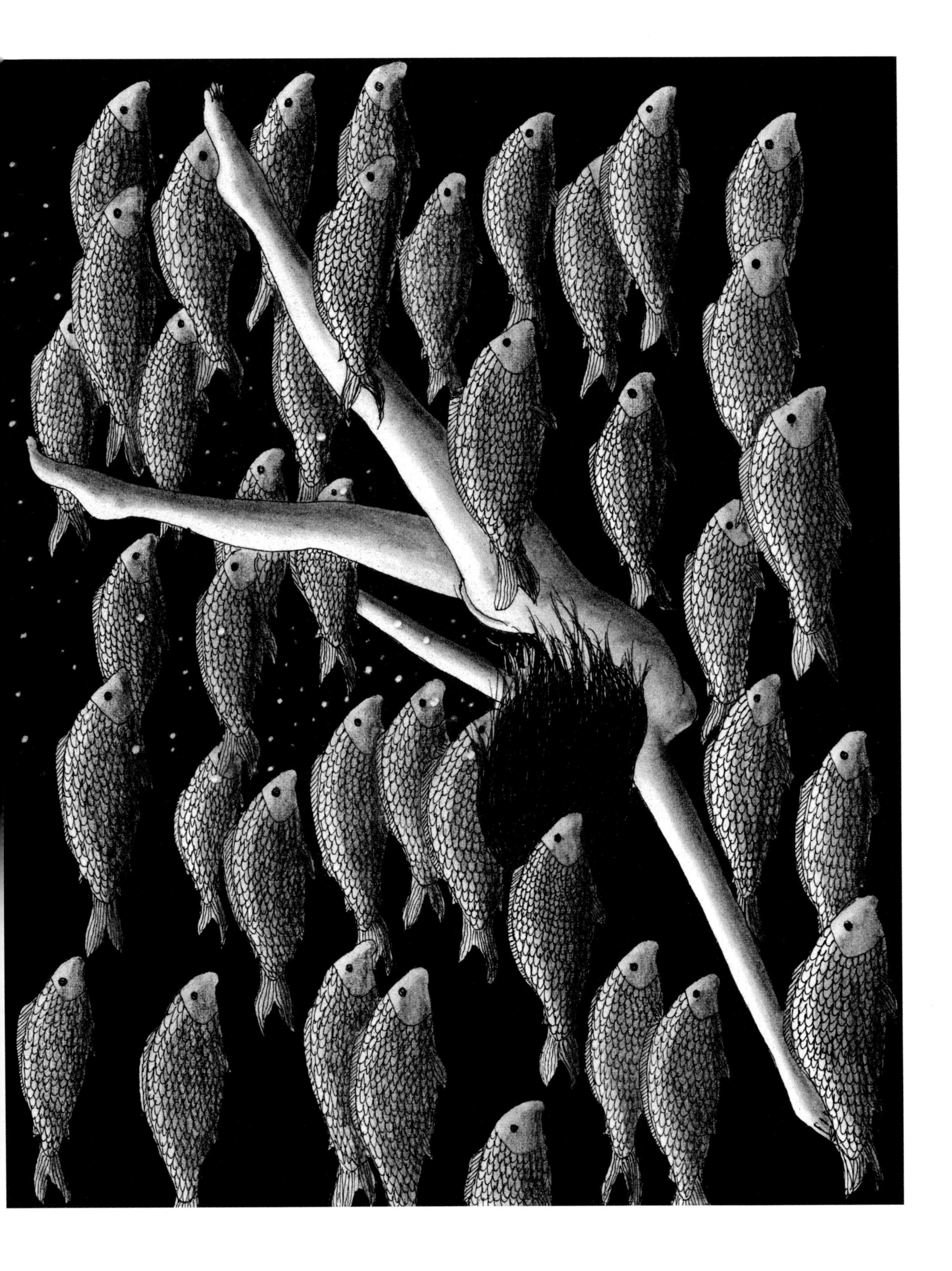

PRIMAL

One of the strangest things I went through was the strong sense
that I had to get in touch with my most primal self.

My original self. My essential self.

Actually, I didn't feel like I had a choice. It was thrust upon me. It was a necessity. No. More than that. It just was. It was meant to be and therefore was.

Integrating our highest selves with our deepest selves is excruciatingly difficult because at first we assume it is not only impossible but wrong.

The challenge is enormous… to get over our fear, our hesitancy, our resistance.

When I fled my captivity, I felt immediate relief.
The space I was in was infinite.
But I did not feel lost within it.
No, the immediate feeling was relief.

Then, realizing there was no one watching with a critical eye,
I let myself fall deep within myself to find what was there.
If I was there.
Or someone else.

It was ancient. Immediate. Primal.

I met my deepest, most ancient self.
My primal self.
My essential self.

For once in my life I felt connected not only to my past but to the past and all that was and all that is and all that will be. For once I felt anchored into the earth and at one with it. For once I felt like a member of the universe and a citizen of the world and a being on the planet and a person on the earth.

I felt… natural.
I felt nurtured by
my most primal self.

Why, when we become more natural, are we accused of giving free rein to our baser instincts? Our primal urges? Our darker drives? In fact I felt more whole, more rounded, more one, more integrated, more human! I was fully me.

Primal. Primary. Prime.

ENTANGLED

Soon after I escaped from whom I thought were my enemies
I discovered I was my own worst enemy.
My escape was a declaration of war on myself.
My past self. My false self. My publicly approved self.
Hand to hand combat in close quarters. Both sides get bruises.
One side wins.
One side loses.

Oh what a bloody war. A war to end all wars! Two superpowers. The conflict was within me. In my own mind. In my own heart. It all took place right here. It wasn't out there. My worst enemy was lurking behind my own eyelids the whole time.

There were days I didn't think I was going to survive.
My enemy… me… used every tactic available.
It followed no protocol.
It obeyed no rules.
It recognized no conventions.

Some days it was guerilla warfare. Some days it was remote warfare. Some days it was slash and burn warfare. Some days it was frontal attack warfare. It has been said that war is boredom punctuated by sheer terror. I know this. It's true!

My enemy was merciless. Therefore so was I.

This was the angriest time of my life. I was angry at my enemies. Angry at life. Ultimately angry at myself.

I could not understand this violent urge to destroy myself. What did I do to provoke myself to such rage and uncontrollable animosity towards myself? Why did I want to make myself suffer so? Why did I demand my own life? To crucify myself?

Why was I so willing to lay down my life? Perhaps to find it.

It reminds me of Jacob wrestling with the angel, which in essence was him wrestling with himself. This is my story.

It is waged in darkness. There is no light.
I am alone. No one can rescue me.
There's a fight. The bitter battle waged within.
I want a blessing. I want something out of this.

Whether they are my inner demons or angels, I cannot tell.
I might walk with a limp. But I'll have won!

REBEL

What an interesting journey! What a fight!

Of course, this drawing conjures up the story of Eve.

Eve ate the forbidden fruit and gained knowledge. Here, Sophia not only takes one bite, but indulges herself. She must know! She needs to understand! She must be herself, fulfill her destiny, and be! She IS. She can say with full confidence, "I AM!" If it takes a rebellion to be able to say this, then so be it!

Didn't one theologian say, "When you sin, sin boldly"? Didn't he also say, "O precious fault'? Eve sinned boldly and committed the precious fault.

I realized when I first started drawing Sophia that I was drawing the journey of my own soul. I guess my soul, whatever that is, identifies itself as feminine. Many women resonate with her. But many men who I suspect are in touch with their feminine side, their anima, appreciate her story as well. We can recognize our own journeys in Sophia's.

It's about empowerment.

When I first made my escape, some thought that this was me suddenly being empowered. No! Actually, my empowerment was gradual, like the dawning of the sun. My escape only demonstrated this empowerment. Now, this empowerment grows and grows and grows.

I can't be stopped.

There is a strong woman within me.

I believe, just from examining myself, that all women are strong, as all souls are strong, and that under the right conditions this strength can grow and demonstrate itself in healthy and diverse ways. I see this happening all the time.

I'm excited about what women are doing and what's going to become of the groundswell of female intelligence and independence.

Because I believe this is a universal kind of spiritual development and advancement.

Sophia is a rebel and leads her own rebellion for her independence and the independence of all others.

And you are a rebel too! If you want to be you, you must be.

NIGHTMARE

Many of us are raised to be at war with ourselves.

Here is a nightmare of mine: disembodiment.
Disintegration.
I don't mean physically.
I mean emotionally, psychologically, spiritually.

I was taught to hate my body.
The flesh.
With all that is associated with it.
Everything natural.

So I grew up divided.
Constantly torn apart.
Always at war with myself.
And losing.
Defeated.

Until I saw we are one.
And that I am one.
With myself!
United.
Whole.
Perfect.
Just as I am.

Sure, I'm aware of this or that part of my nature that I am not pleased with.
But now I see it is as a smaller part of a greater fabric of my story.

Now that which I see in my darkness is not something I must kill,
but integrate. This is how I am whole. This is how I am one.

That which is not true I let pass through. That which is true remains.

I simply don't accept divisive words anymore. I don't believe lies about my partiality,
my imperfection, my brokenness, my divided self.

These are illusions. Like a dream. Like nightmares.

When one is fully awake one sees all things as one.
One sees all things as perfect. Every single thing.
Including me.

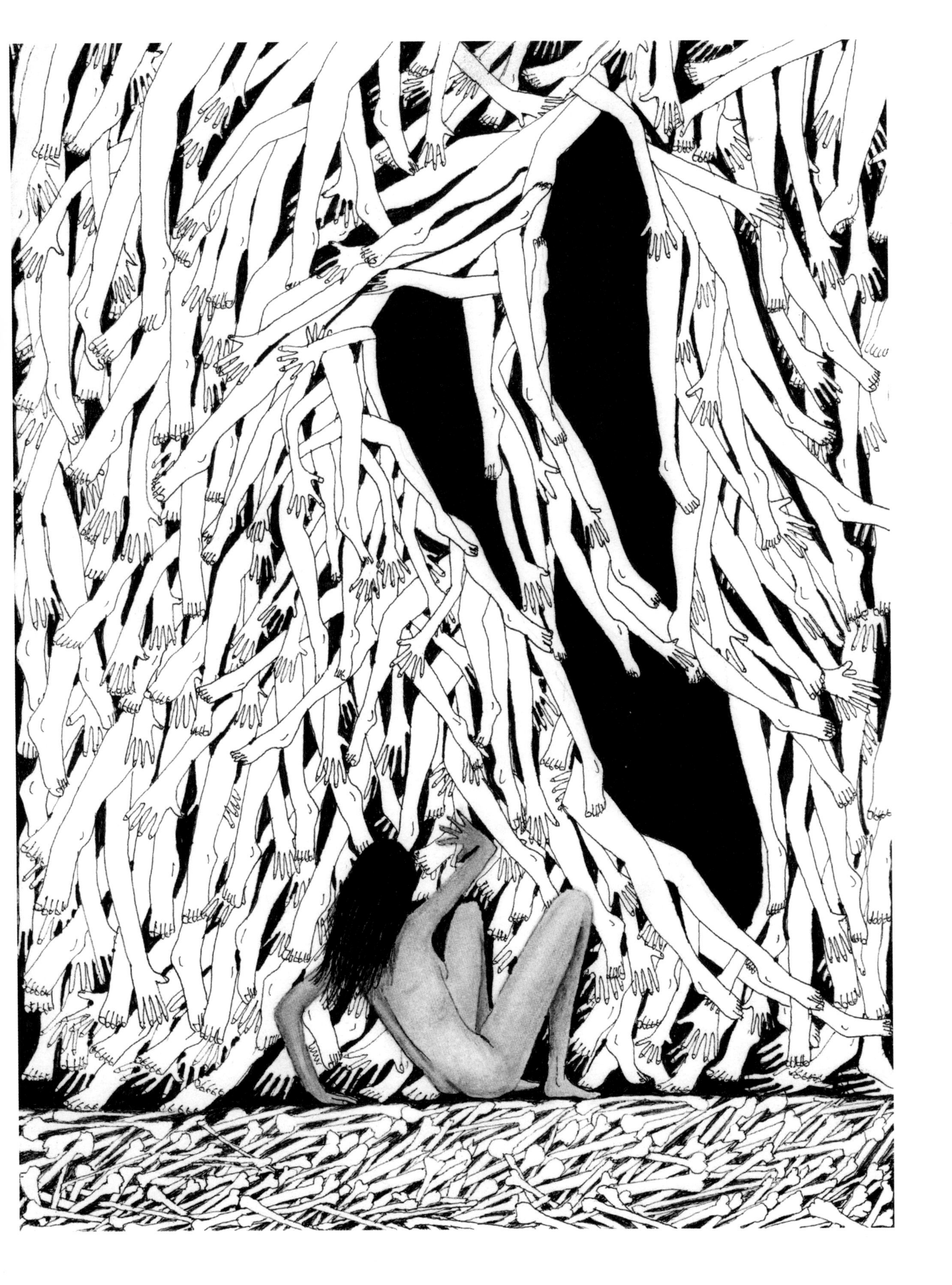

DEEP

Although words that were meant to be holy
have been used to hurt me,
I still love some of them.

I see their original beauty.

I love this from the Psalms:

"Deep calls to deep in the thunder of your waterfalls."

I've always felt the call to go deeper. As deep as possible.

I read depth-psychology. Philosophy. Theology. Mysticism.
I immersed myself in all these.

Even in my imprisonment I practiced prayer, meditation, contemplation, thinking, spiritual direction, keeping a journal…
all things that tend to pull you deeper into the deepest depths.
If you allow them.

Help came along through mysterious means.

Loons.

I remember once being on a windsurfing board on a calm lake. I was reading the theologian Tillich at the time. He was pulling me through very deep waters. As I was standing on this board in the middle of the lake, no wind, I noticed this very large black and white shape glide underneath me and my board.

Remember my fear of deep water?
And the mysterious things that lurk beneath?

It was a loon. I couldn't believe how big it was. I wasn't aware that loons were so big. They are amazing swimmers and can descend into the depths. They can also fly very high. The loon filled me with terror and wonder all at once. Like theology.

It was at once frightening and mystical.

Loons are nature's mystics.
But, like the loon,
what drew me deeper would also take me higher.

I knew this.

CLEANSED

After I escaped I felt like I could shower forever.

I mean, in one way I felt clean like I'd shaken off the dirt.
In another way I felt filthy with stuff I couldn't somehow shake.

It was the residue of all my years of slavery
and my necessary collusion with it.

I forgive myself. I did it in order to survive.

What's been done to me
and what I've done to myself. I forgive.
What I've been given
and what I've received. I forgive.

It hasn't all been good.
It's all been… questionable.

But here I feel the glue
of all that residue
gathered over the years
sticking to my body,
my bones,
my soul.

I've been caught in a rain storm. I've fallen to the ground. I will let it all soak in.

My many years of servitude,
my years of compromise,
my years of confusion,
my years of captivity,
my years of fear.

May they all drain out of me
and into the ground
to bury themselves.
I've never felt this clean,
this pure,
this complete.

I'll remember this rainy night…
my truest baptism.

CROUCH

Sometimes I find myself in the strangest positions.
Sometimes I get myself in the strangest positions.
Sometimes I put myself in the strangest positions.

I crouch for two reasons:
To make myself smaller to hide or defend,
or to prepare for my next move and pounce!

There's nothing wrong with making yourself smaller to hide. Even the fiercest fighters defend.

Believe me: I fight fiercely most of the time.
But every once in a while I just need a break.
Every once in a while I have to pull back, pull in and crouch.
Just to catch my breath.
Just to relax my intensity.
Just to regain my strength.

Then there are times when I need to prepare myself for what's next.
There are times when I have to just stop, store up some energy, and strike forth!
I relax my muscles and recoil them in an explosive surge forward.
Sure, sometimes my movement is gradual.
But sometimes it's sudden and instantaneous.
When I see the next thing I have to do I prepare.
Then I pounce!

Others wonder what's going on with me when I crouch. I hear it in their words of concern. "You seem quiet lately." "You're usually so intense." "Why have you stopped?" "What's going on? Why aren't you as aggressive as usual?"

Between my movements are commas that look like comas.
I just stop.
I curl up.
I rest.
I wait.

A thousand mile journey begins with the first step.
I take ground by inches. But I take ground!

I'm an encroacher. Just as sudden as I pulled back, I pounce forward.

And I'm back in the game.

RESONANCE

Captivity colors your world.
It taints it.
Stains it.

It can make you feel small in a small world.
It can make you feel out of sync with the universe.
It can make you feel restricted in a restrictive world.
It can make you feel less than human.

The strange thing is you know you are human,
but you don't feel it.
You feel dehumanized.

Like a prisoner, you feel separated from the real, the natural, the free.
You even feel separated from your own body. Divided.

All your time and energy is spent supporting a machine that claims to support you. But you can never disconnect from the machine or the support it promises. That's the cost.

It was a gamble cutting myself
away from the machine.
What if its claims were true?
What if its threats had substance?
But I had to escape to find out.
I couldn't stand not knowing.

So one of the first things I felt after my escape was, well, natural.

Nature has a way with me. We resonate. It is in nature that I feel human. I feel like a person at one with the earth. From earth I came, to earth I will return. Because I am the earth! What a better way to become harmonious. To be in nature.

I walk through the forest.
I feel the breeze and see the moonlight on my skin.
The earth beneath my feet.
The smells.
These round me out. They fulfill me.

Somehow I feel completed,
for I resonate with nature
and it resonates with me.

WAITING

I taught myself the art of waiting.

I waited for the perfect time to escape.

But I was learning before then. One of the things captivity uses on you is rationing. Restraints. In a sense I always had to wait. So I made it a skill.

The temptation is always to settle. Like a sly lawyer, it coaxes you into taking an offer because the best settlement is not guaranteed.

Waiting is considered a stupid move.
Or selfish.
Or both.

I've given in many times. I still do. I still may.
I'm not sure why. Perhaps these are moments of weakness.

I should know better.

Because it's proven itself to me over and over again.
It's proven that the best will come if you wait for it.
And if it doesn't come the waiting has changed your heart for something better.

Waiting, therefore, is a permanent thing.
It is a way of being.
It is a form of contentment.
It is a form of desire.
Not the desire that drives one to death,
but the kind of desire that rests with itself.
And waits. Contented.
It is a peaceful posture.

The bright moon in the dark night reminds me of this.
I stand alone with the moon.
The light of the night.
I settle for that.
But it holds a promise.
A promise that is actually fulfilled.
It promises that the light that illumines it
is just upon us.

I'll wait for that.

SURRENDER

Sometimes I had to just surrender. I don't mean to the enemy. I mean to what is.

Surrender to what is. Not like a victim. But like a participant. Like a lover.

Like floating.

Floating is very active. It is not passive at all. It requires poise, patience, some knowledge and skill, and, finally, trust.

Trust.

I think people fall into two categories: one is they generally feel the world is against them, and the other feels the world is for them. I'm not sure of this. Someone might be slightly more than the other. But I suspect we all fall into one camp or the other.

I've been in both. Living in captivity eroded my trust. I let it.

Then, at some point in my captivity, I knew I had to rekindle trust. I actually remember the day I realized that I was waiting to be rescued, when all I had to do was surrender to what is, to trust what is, and be transformed.

My chains were broken before I broke them.

Trust:
I myself had uprooted it.
So I myself had to replant it.
It wasn't a pessimistic "You made your bed. Now sleep in it."
It was a optimistic "Here's freedom's door. Now walk through it."

It wasn't done for me. I had to do it for myself. But the call to do it empowered me. When a player wins, the coach is praised as well. Likewise, the call, like a coach, empowered me to surrender and trust that I was cared for. I can't explain it. It is a sense that I still carry.

It took a lot of work.
But I have surrendered.

And I discovered I am cared for.

GRATEFUL

I am grateful.

I'll admit something.
While I was in my captivity I thought I was grateful.
When you are a slave you appreciate your rations.

You're grateful for
the little you get to eat;
the little you get to do;
the little you get to be.

For me, nights are the moments most filled with benediction.
Especially when the moon is out.

So I raise my hands.
It is just a gesture.
It isn't really planned.
There is no one up there, seated in the heavens, looking down.
There is no separation.

But I do it anyway.
Maybe this comes from my past.
Maybe within me dwells a liturgist.
Maybe I'm part priest.

I used to pray differently.
As if to something. Or someone.
But now I utter thanks.
For I am grateful to the One
of which I am.

Mysteriously,
I wrought my escape with my own hands,
and with my own hands I built my home here.

But at the same time I know it is all a gift…
that it has come to me,
and that I am being given it.

So I open my arms to receive it.
And I'm grateful.

BRANCHING

I used to live such a small life. Limited. Confined. Petty.
I must have been unconscious most of the time.

But like a wild animal caged for a long, long time that smells the expansive, distant wilderness in the breeze, I occasionally sensed that something was amiss. At the time you can't really tell what it is. Or if anything's missing.
You can't know what you don't know.
You can't remember what you've never experienced.

You're taught that you're being greedy.
Or that you're just in a rush.
Or that you should be faithful in little
before you can be faithful in much.

We are told and required to be content with what we have.

So all our world
and all our dreams
close in on us
and become lean.

But when I liberated myself
and sank my roots deeper than deep,
I let them nourish me
and I quickly branched out in all directions.

Freedom isn't just an idea.
It's not just a condition.
It's freedom of thought.
Freedom of speech.
Freedom of movement.

It's like my curiosity burst at the seams.
I no longer hid my light under a bushel.
And all other lights were not hid from me.
I discovered that I could branch out anywhere
and gather nourishment from everywhere.

My manifold branches reaching out in manifold directions
demonstrated the spread of my roots and I revealed my glory.

I would grow large! Nothing was restricted to me anymore. To the pure all things are pure.

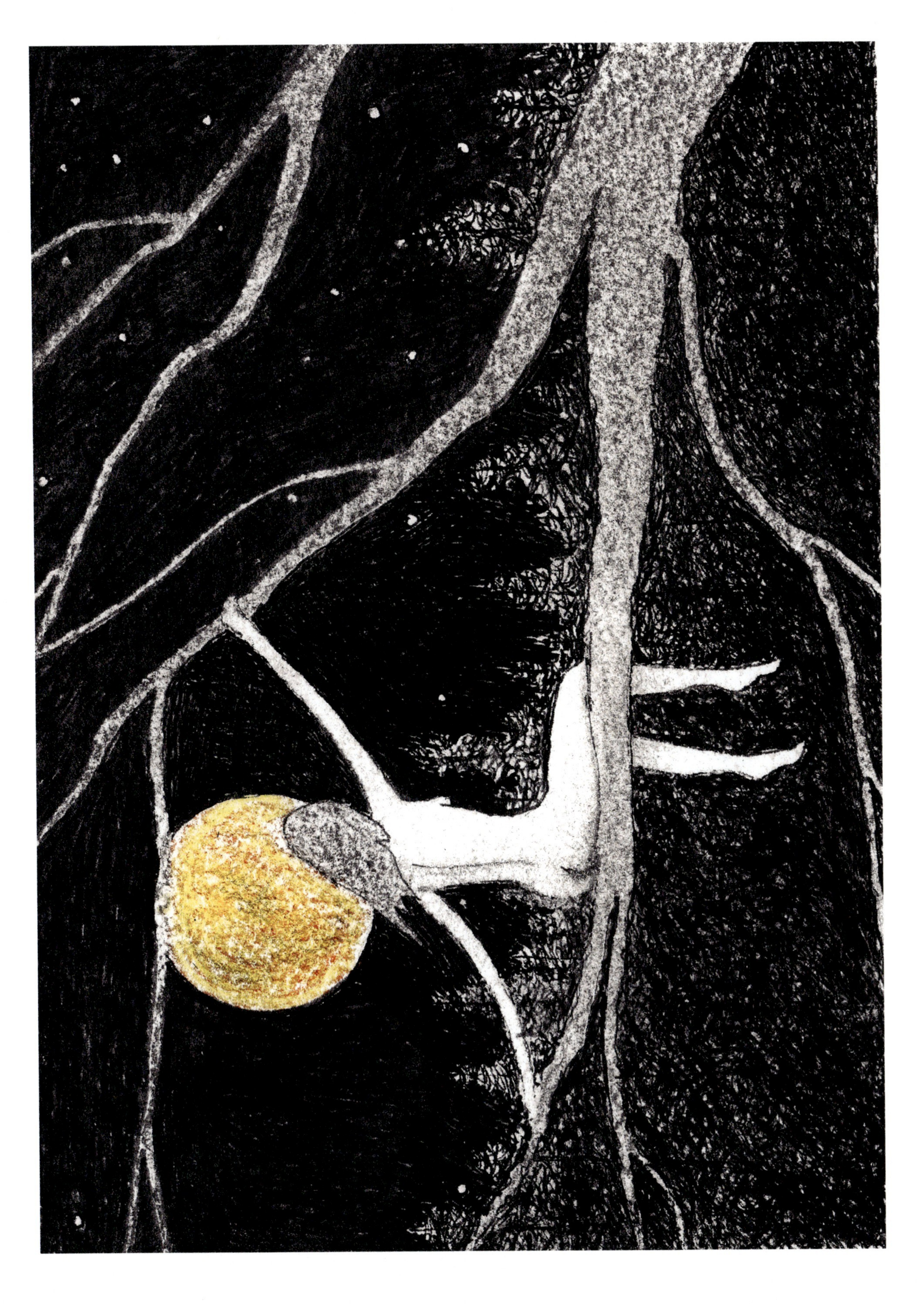

TRANSPARENT

I don't mean to offend you by my transparency. That's your problem. Not mine.

I have to say that a lot.

I am transparent.
This offends people.

But look at me. I'm beautiful. You are looking at me, and yet you are looking through me at the moon. You are looking through me at everything.

I am so one with everything that the more transparent I am the more of everything lays before your eyes. I am a portal into all things.

And so are you!

I am told people can see right through me and that this makes me shallow. Not true! This means I am more complex.

What is more mysterious? To try to look through a wall to the other side? Or to look through a glass darkly? It is not having it that is more powerful, but the desire for it. It's not seeing it all that is most striking, but wanting to see more that is more powerful.

This is why some say I'm so open and others say I'm so mysterious. It is because I'm transparent. Mystery confounds people.

It is impossible for people to completely know me. I don't even completely know myself. So I'm not afraid of being transparent with people because I draw from a fathomless well.

The more transparent I am
the more deep I am
and the more mystifying I am.

You look down a well and you see water. You see that the water is clear. It is transparent. It is clean. But you can't see that the well is deep beyond measure.

That is just like me. This is just like you.

Of myself I hoard nothing. And this makes me greater.
As great as the whole wide universe. Even infinite.

Of myself I give and give and give, totally open and transparent, and it is exactly this that makes my supply infinite. I am transparent.

CANOE

In my escape from my imprisonment, I came across this abandoned canoe. So I took it. I took advantage of it. I used it.

It was there and I let it help me.

I let it assist me on my journey.

Something that I've learned along the way is this:
it is important, wise, and frugal to take advantage of anything
that presents itself as help.
I've learned to make use of whatever is available to assist.
And my help came from very unexpected places.

Before, what I could use on my journey was very particular.

There were rules.
Laws.
Expectations.
Protocols.
Standards.
Traditions.

But when I escaped it was from those I escaped. There's nothing wrong with tradition. In fact, I appreciate tradition. I have found much tradition very rich and meaningful. However, when tradition becomes the prevention of freedom, another cell, then it has misused its power. Like an overbearing mother.

Anchors are good unless you want to sail.

So I have found help in all kinds of other places that weren't allowed or even considered before. Sometimes I use them by stealth. Other times I use them openly.

I found myself doing things like reading, listening to, enjoying, consuming, partaking, attending… things I would have never even considered before or ever been caught using. Now there is no one looking over my shoulder judging me for what I use to help me on my journey. I'm free to use any resource that makes itself available to me.

If it's useful then I will use it.

If it's going to help me grow, mature, become wise, travel well, and be free, then I will use it.

Like this canoe.

STUDY

I've always read. I've always studied. I've always been curious.

Here, after my escape, in the middle of the wilderness, all alone, I find books in an ancient, abandoned library. I study. I voraciously devour it all.

I used to be told what to believe and what to read. But I would read what interested me and it got me into frequent trouble.
Now I read and study what I want and nobody can say anything.
They can't threaten me with the loss of my job,
or my security,
or my place,
or my salvation.

I need to know, and I need to know for myself. I have no problem with adopting thoughts. But I do want to shape some thoughts of my own.

I've discovered a beautiful thing:
Truth is not contained.
Truth is not controlled.
Truth is like air.
It is everywhere. There is no road to it. We're already there.
Even when some try to restrict it,
it won't take long to burst out of its cage.

Even in opposing systems of thought, there's truth in each. It demands to be known.

I have the truth already within me. If I was wise enough I would see it, past all the accretions I've gathered over the years. Like finding an ancient holy temple deep in a jungle overgrown with vines. It is there, just concealed. Truth is like that within me. And within you.

So I study to find out what this truth looks like
so that I'll recognize it when I see it.
And I've discovered that the truth that is within me
resonates with the truth that I read, so that when those two conjoin
there is another installment
in my temple of wisdom.

I study everything.
I study to show myself approved.
It's not how I became wise, for I was wise already.
As Socrates said.
It is proof of my wisdom.

BALANCE

I lost my balance.

I lost it.
Something that is mine.
Something I could find and recover.

Like a level, balance was always within me.
It was always there.
I had lost my balance…
the balance I needed to find.

I knew this meant I was out of touch with myself.

Then, when I escaped my captivity,
for a while I really lost my balance.
I mean I was completely unbalanced. I lost plumb.
People noticed.

Those who loved me most
had the love and courage
to tell me I needed to find my balance. To find plumb.

I knew they were right. I knew I had lost it.

So I took advantage of my few loved ones, my family and friends.
I also found a person who was very wise that I could talk to.
I unearthed good books.
If I hadn't done this
I would have crashed.
I think I would have fallen forever.
I believe I would have vanished.

Instead, I found the balance I finally needed.
The balance that was always inside me
waiting to find plumb.

The greatest spiritual teachers are right.
Peace is not found in excess.
Neither is it found in austerity.
It is found in between.
For I am neither there nor there nor there.
I am here. Now.

CONQUER

Fear.
The greatest obstacle.

Where does fear reside?
In my mind.
Only.

Along with my fear of deep water comes my fear of sharks.
A reasonable fear.

The deep represents my most mysterious self that is hidden in darkness.
I'm taking care of that.

The shark represents my enemies, those who would stalk, circle, and devour me.
I need to take care of this.
But I won't deal with my enemies, but my fear of them.

I will conquer this fear.

So I put myself through a contemplative exercise.
An imaginary devotional.

I grab a lasso and slip into the surf.
I will face my fear of the enemy.

Why a lasso?

Because I've come to believe that there are only two ways to eliminate an enemy:
Push them away. Hate them.
Bring them closer. Love them.

With the first, you must also lose yourself.
With the second, you must also love yourself.

I chose the second.

So to conquer this fear I will draw the enemy close.

I have decided that since I love myself...

I will also love my enemy.
I have conquered my fear.

FEARLESS

The revelation dawned on me one morning after I awakened from a dream.

I am a child again.

I am alone again in the wilderness.

I come across a large bear. I startle him.
He startles me.

He rises on his haunches and stands like a giant in the land.

I am so very small.

You know how dreams work.
Somehow I know that this bear is me.
I hold up my teddybear as a gesture of peace.

We stare at each other for a long time.
I cannot count the minutes.
My heart is racing.

He sniffs the air.
He looks at me intently.
I look back gently.

Finally he falls back on all fours and wanders down the hill into the deep, dark forest. I am at peace with my inner beast.

I grew up with the idea that I was inherently weak. Broken. Sinner. But I secretly knew that within me was a bear. I had the strength of a bear lurking deep in my inner cave. I was wild, strong and free.

My strength was hibernating in wait for the spring of my liberation.

It would come forth fearless.
Not that I would never be afraid, but that my courage, like a beast,
would overcome and keep me on my path heading toward my goal.

I would not only surprise others.
I would surprise myself.

I am fearless!

MIGHT

Oh the strength!

The strength that is within me.

I can do all things.

Not by might. Not by power. But by spirit!

It's not like it's my might.
It's when I'm in touch with what is true,
with what is spirit,
that this might courses through me.
I will not lay claim to this power.
But it has laid claim to me.

I dreamed I had a staff. Like Moses'. I didn't part a sea, but I stopped a herd of elephants. I stopped giants in their tracks. I know how unreasonable it sounds. I know how dangerous it looks. Careless. Death-defying.

I've heard that it is not the darkness within us that we fear, but the light. We are frightened by our own light. We are afraid to shine our light to those around us. We shrink back, intimidated by our light and the effect it has on the world. We are afraid of our own power.

You see me there, so small in the face of such a moving mass.
But I trusted in the sense of spirit that reverberates within me.

It took a lot of courage for me to escape.
Then to separate myself.
Then to distinguish myself.

Some thought I was being a fool.
Some thought my risks were senseless.
Some thought I had lost my mind.
Some thought I had betrayed the holy.

True. The change in me was cataclysmic. It quaked the earth beneath my feet and those near me felt it rumble.

The change in me changed everything around me. The world changed.

And I proved that when I am in touch with spirit I can do all things.
I proved it. I can change. I can bring change. I can do all things.

I live in a transformed and transforming world.

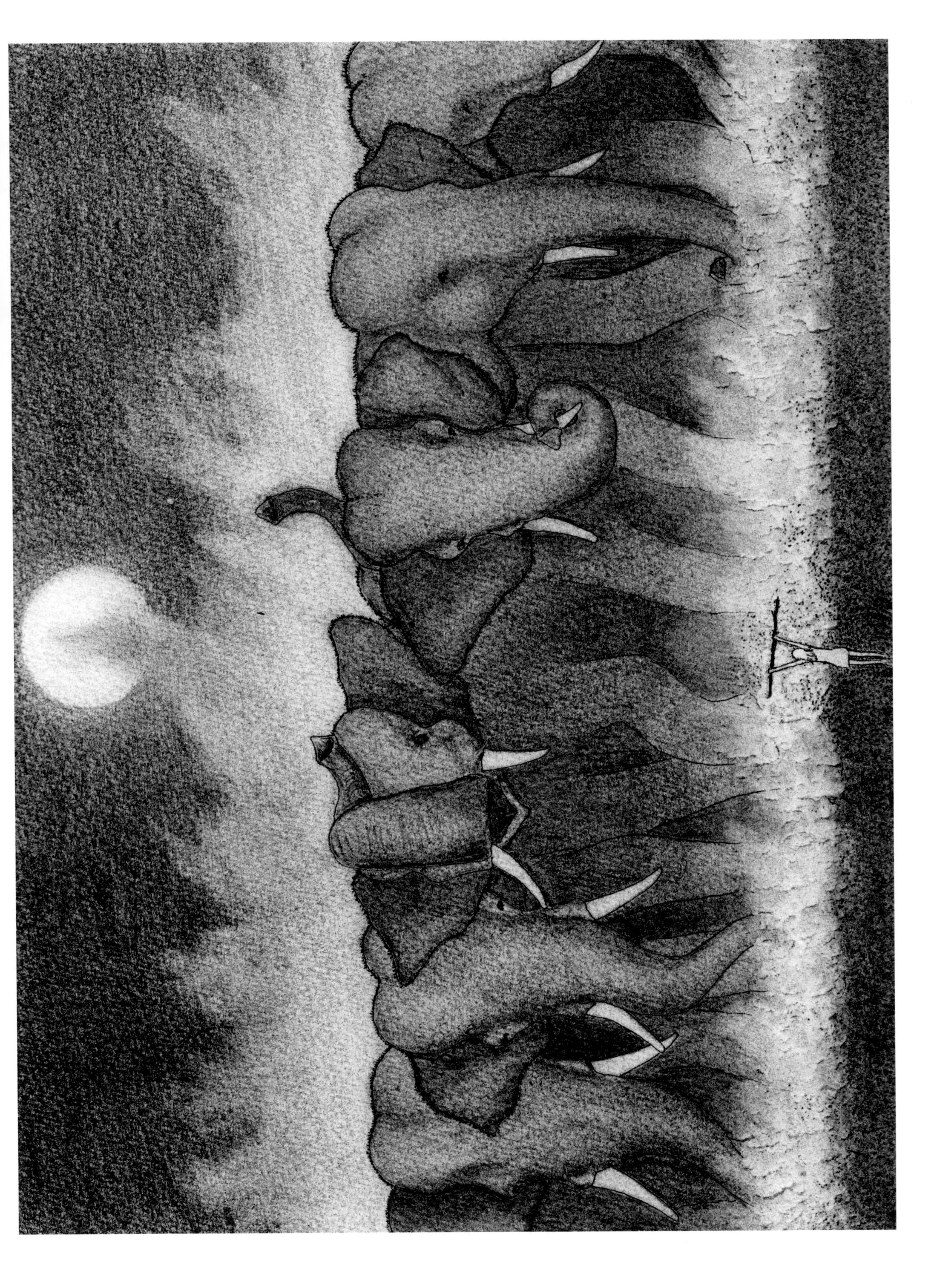

STEADFAST

The hardest thing for me to do
was to remain steadfast.

To keep my feet on my own path was sometimes nearly impossible.
I was ready to quit as many times as I was ready to move on.

I'm not sure if my resolve is sandwiched between my indecision
or if my indecision is sandwiched between my resolve.
In the end it didn't matter because I did stand my ground.
I remained steadfast.

Here I stand before a rhinoceros, an immovable mass.
But with just the slightest gesture I stand my ground.
I touch his nose.

So many things tried to
dissuade me,
discourage me,
disparage me,
distract me.

Family. Friends. Fears. Finances. You name it.

Sometimes, like this small child, I felt like I was all alone in all the universe,
and that I had to resist, every day, every temptation, to give up, to let the weight of the world crush me.

Once you embark on this road, there can be no turning back.
And there can be no turning aside.
I realized that once I set my face like a flint towards my own Jerusalem,
I had to keep my focus, keep my bearings, and keep my feet upon my path.

To go back would have killed me.
To turn aside would have derailed me.
I wouldn't have become the me that I am.
And always was.

To abort my mission was not an option.
I stood my ground!

I am steadfast.
And steadfast still.

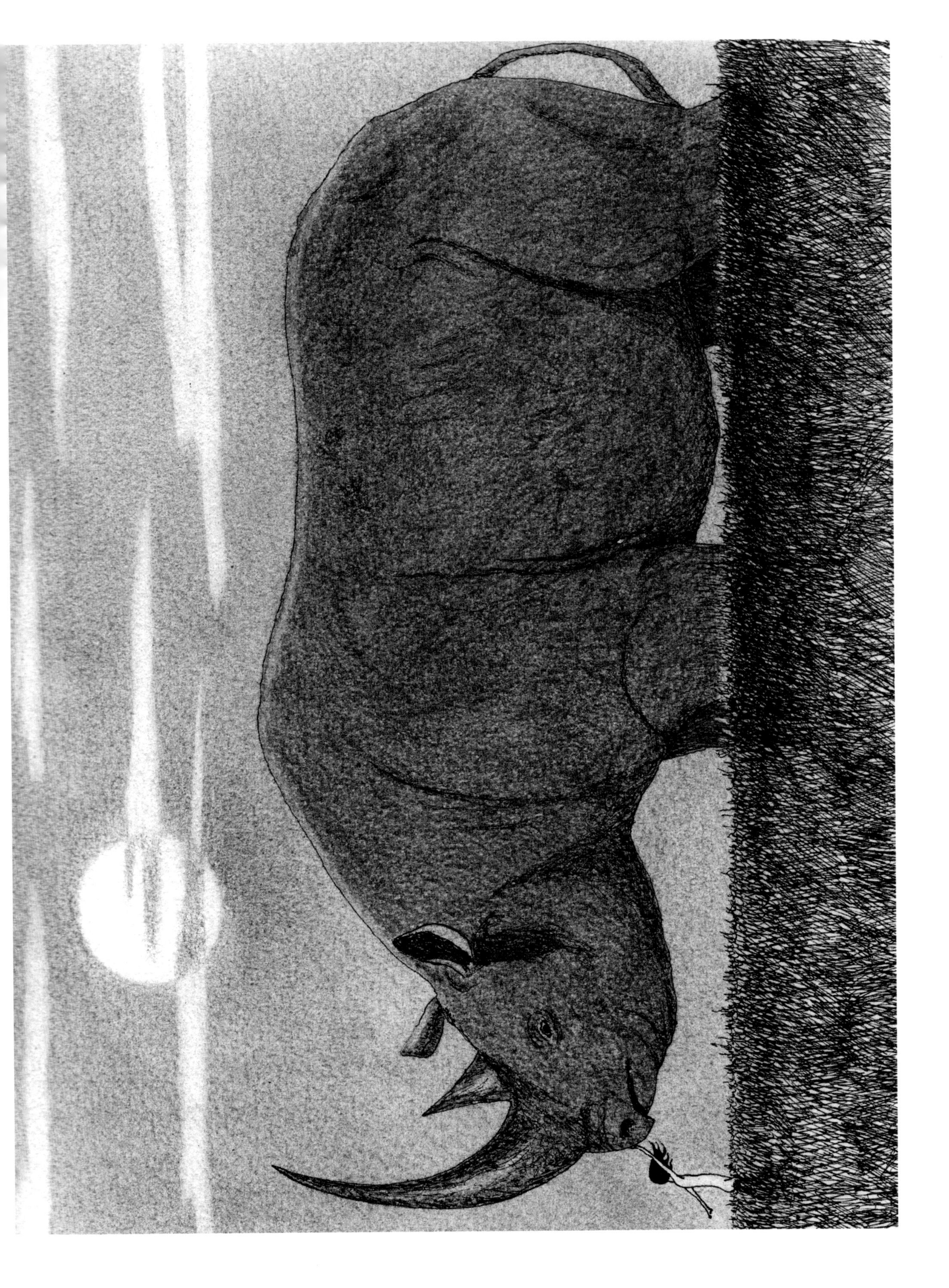

AGREEMENT

How can such a young, vulnerable person like me come to an agreement with such a powerful and wild animal?

I had to make an agreement.

With myself.

With my wild self.

I made an agreement to live at peace with myself.

I made an agreement to live at peace with every part of myself. I brought the tame and the wild together.

Like with this wild cat, I came to an agreement with;
my fierce independence
and
my need to hunt.

It took me a long time to come to know, love and appreciate the wild, untamable animal within me. For I needed this to find my own food. To take care of myself.

I came to respect and fear this wild part of myself.

It took me even longer to reveal it. To release it.

I do not wait for others to accept it or not. This is who I am.

But at least now they know:

I shall not be tamed.
I shall not be messed with.
I shall not stop hunting.

For I have entered into an agreement.
With myself.
With all of myself.

I am wild.
I am fierce.
I am independent.
I am a hunter.

I will find what I'm hunting for.

SHELTER

Even though I was exposed to the elements, I did find places of shelter.

I love shelter.

What was a strange revelation to me was that where I found the best shelter
was under that which is ancient.
Things that have been true forever.

Ancient wisdom.

Strange, isn't it?

Some of the very things I thought I wanted to escape from became my shelter.

Marriage.
Family.
Community.
Me.
My body with its needs and desires.
And yes, even my religion with its writings.
The ancient wisdom and traditions that survived the centuries.
Not all of it, but what is true about them.

Here is where I found my shelter.

Things that have been proven by people just like me for thousands of years.

Yes, the storms of my life would assail me.
But these come and go.

Storms are the weather. They aren't the climate.

Storms are anomalies.

But I found shelter in that which was deep, founded, and sure.
What is true has always been true and always will be true.

Yes, I discarded all that had been added onto these things that weren't true.
But these things stripped down to their essentials are strong and sure.

I'm thankful for the gift of shelter.
Just when I needed it.

ROOTED

I examined my roots.
Anything that was dead I laid the axe to.
Anything that had life I let live.

For a long time I wanted to reject all my roots.
I harbored an incredible amount of resentment toward them.
Even disdain.

I wanted to be completely free. At first we experience confusion about how that is done and what that looks like. I thought that in order to fully ascend I needed to completely detach myself from everything that bound me to the earth.

I made the mistake of thinking that
in order to run free
I should neglect that which fed me.
My center. My roots.

I equated my roots with bondage. Something that kept me earth bound. Anchors.

There was the temptation to cut myself off from everything. Some of it was dead roots. But I was tempted to indiscriminately cut off even those that were giving me life. There was resentment that, even though I was totally free, I was still in some ways bound. Held responsible.

My body needed things. I needed security. I needed love. I needed purpose. I even needed me. This was the crux! I needed me. I couldn't escape myself. Wherever I go, there I am.

I run. Once when I was running I realized that I am earthbound as much as I am airborne. Without both I couldn't run. That's what running is. So I conceded: the deeper my roots the higher my reach. Like this great tree in the forest. See how high it rises! It even reaches up to the moon. But it couldn't do this without its majestic roots that sink deep into the earth. The earth that I wanted to escape.

Yes, I wanted to rise up into the heavens. But I couldn't without sinking deep into the earth. I would be a human being… only a little lower than the angels. So I embraced my roots. I studied them. In fact I fed them Because they would in turn feed me. Jung said that no tree can grow to heaven unless its roots reach down to hell.

You might look upon me as wild and uncontrolled. And I am!
But have you seen my roots? This is what feeds my freedom.

I fly. But I am rooted.

LONGING

As deer long for fresh water, so I long for what is true.

Desire is strange.
Longing is mysterious.
Wanting is perplexing.

On the one hand I grasp the necessity of contentment.
On the other hand I grasp the necessity of change.
I was told I had everything I needed.
I thought therefore that I had everything I wanted.

The hardest question for me to ever answer was, "What do you want?" It was impossible to reply. I didn't know what I wanted. I only knew what everyone else wanted. In wanting to give them everything I gave them nothing.

Especially me!
In meeting their needs I withheld myself from them.
Because I withheld myself from myself.

Then one day I awakened to realize that my contentment was my captors'.
My contentment was actually a paralysis.
It was a coping mechanism for my powerlessness.

As soon as I realized this I was empowered.
So I decided to embrace it and broke free.
I stood for myself.
I proclaimed, "This is me! And this is what I want!"

Finally I feel my own hunger!
Finally I taste my own thirst!

I still haven't found what I'm looking for. I've been looking for a long time. Therefore, I conclude, that searching is our default setting. When I came to peace with this, I found true peace.

The search is the goal.
There is no path to somewhere.
The path is the destination.

Now I am at once hungry and full.
Thirsty and satisfied.
Searching and finding.
Content and changing.

WISDOM

If you look for wisdom you'll find it.

I've always wanted to be wise.

I didn't realize I would find wisdom when I felt most foolish.

I was just in the dark.

But this is always the case.

Owls are solitary. Nocturnal. They get what they want by stealth and surprise.

That's an accurate description of me.

Owls are also sometimes associated with wisdom. I'm not sure why. Perhaps because they can see in the darkness. Perhaps because they are like lonely hermits. Perhaps because they are patient. Perhaps because they are effective hunters. Perhaps all these things.

Alone. In darkness. This is where I find my wisdom.

Why is it that when I was in my captivity, surrounded by what they called light, swimming in books, drowning in words, and choking on a never-ending stream of ideas, that wisdom eluded me? Why is it when am most secure I am most blind?

You can't hunt in your own house.
You must slip by night into the wilderness.
That's where the prey is. That's where your desire lies waiting.

Every breakthrough followed a breakout.
And every breakout followed a breakthrough.

Freedom begets wisdom, and wisdom begets freedom.

One of the wisest things I know I will now share with you: I carry with me all that I was and all that I am and all that I will be. Everything I experienced, the good and the bad, everything I've learned, everything, my whole history, my whole story, my whole universe and yours, this is who I am. The All in All. I carry it within me. As me.

For I Am.

Everything is. And I love it. As I love myself.

This is my wisdom. And yours.

PROVISION

There is a story of a hungry man who sought and spoke truth being fed by ravens.

The hardest lesson for me to learn was the lesson of provision.

I've always struggled with money. Money and I always fought ever since I was a kid. I'm not sure why. There can be a myriad of reasons. But even though I always had just enough, it always seemed dangerously close to the edge. I was always on the narrow path between not enough and just enough.

The spiritual milieu I found myself in nurtured this meager mentality. It kept me subservient. It cultivated a slave attitude within me. It enabled my victimhood. I was always needy. I was always looking for rescue.

Then I noticed something. I noticed that my spiritual sensitivity to not give money power actually gave money the same power another way. To say "Money, I need you!" is just the opposite side of the coin of pow to say "Money, I don't need you!"

So I was victimizing myself.

I learned that it is all about provision.
I will be provided for.
I always have and I always will.

I do realize that this is one of the most frightening things that prevents many people from making their escap and exercising their freedom. I knew this because I knew this fear myself. But the many breakthroughs that I've made proved each and every time that even though I didn't see my provision yet, it always eventually showed up. I'm painfully aware that every time was a risk. But I'm joyfully aware, every time, it was a surpris

I stepped out of a guaranteed security that was my prison
into a guaranteed insecurity that was my provision. Every. Time.

Provision comes. And it often comes in surprising ways. Not through the usually expected means.

Somehow, I became certain that I was cared for.
Somehow, I became certain that when I made steps towards exercising my freedom and pursuing truth that provision would fly my way.

Now I'm certain of that certainty.
I'm still here, am I not?

SUMMIT

Who shall ascend the hill?
I will!

If I'm not falling, I'm climbing.
I'm getting closer to the peak.
To the top.
To the summit.

It is always a long and treacherous climb because of the night and my vulnerability. Never mind the judgme
of others.

But it is my courage, the sense of urgent necessity, that drives me. Alone. I have no idea what or who awaits me at the summit. But I sense it is Ultimate. And it's probably me.

It will have been worth it all.

I used to just go around and around the base of the mountain looking up at the summit and think I was making progress just because there was a change of scenery. Then then I noticed that I was seeing the same things over and over again. I finally admitted I was really going nowhere.

That's when I started climbing upward.

It is an inward journey with outward manifestations.
It means being myself.
It means knowing myself.
It means loving myself.

I remember the morning I awakened after a dream and I realized I had reached the summit. Actually, the summit is nowhere in particular, yet it sees over everything. I realized the summit was here the whole time. It subsumes everything. It gathers up the All and the All is gathered up under it and into it. It is simply the pinnacle of all that already is.

From the summit I could see, embrace and love all that was and is and shall be... all that was me and is me and shall be me. On the summit I saw that I had scaled all that is. But I also saw that the summit couldn't be the summit without all that is. The summit is a part of the whole. The top of the whole. It is the ultimate glorious manifestation of all that is. It is the height of all things.

So it is not separate. It is not up there. It is not removed. It is where everything is unified in one place. Withi
myself I climb.

DECONSTRUCTION

I've grabbed a sledgehammer
and returned to this wall
to practice a bit of deconstruction.
I'm going to take it down.
Stone by stone.

This is what I do.
There is a time to build
and a time to tear down.
There is a time to plant
and a time to uproot.
It's tearing down time.
It's uprooting time.
It's deconstruction time!

This is the way I see it:
By far the largest part of the problem is the hindrances, barriers, preventions, restrictions, laws, rules, expectations, lies, ideologies, propaganda, assumptions, controls, fences and walls. These are almost all of the problem.

The seed of truth is planted.
The problem is all the stones, lack of nutrients, the weeds, the pests, the weather. There is nothing wrong with the seed or the plant.
What's wrong is all that would hinder or destroy it.

Consider how much more time and effort is involved in weeding than planting.

All these things combine to diminish the human spirit.
So almost all of my time is spent
weeding gardens
and tearing down walls.

Some think
I'm a vandal.
A delinquent.
A saboteur.
But I've become an expert deconstructionist.
I know how to take apart falsehoods and lies and deceptions.
I know how to clear the way for truth to abound.
I've used my skills on myself.
So now I can help others.
I help people deconstruct. That's what I do.

FREEDOM

The taste of freedom is addictive. Once you have it you must have it.

Actually, something I realized while in captivity was that I was always free.

Within.

I had a dream one night during a time when I was feeling the intensity of my captivity more than ever befor
I had fallen into a deep depression, completely hopeless of any liberation.

I couldn't eat.
I couldn't sleep.
I couldn't talk.
I couldn't even live.

In my captivity I was the poorest of prisoners.

But I had a dream.
A simple dream.
All I heard were the words, "It's time!"
That was it. That's all it was.

I woke myself up laughing. It made no sense. But I realized, without there being any external changes at all, that I was free. Totally free. The liberation I was waiting for was already mine. I just needed to live it out. So I did. And free I was!

Is it possible that when I realize I am free within then this freedom works from the inside out and demands, eventually, to be manifested externally? I don't know. I'm just asking. Because this has consistently been my experience. I didn't escape, then realized I was free. I didn't get free, then realized I was free. It is always in this order: I realize I'm free, then my freedom appears.

Now that I am completely free, inside and out, I want others to realize and experience and live their freedom

Free people free others!

Like these horses. I let them go. They were wild. Wild but in a corral. I broke the corral. I let down a rail. Just a rail they could snap in an instant. Immediately, they saw that the only thing separating them from the wild wide open was nothing.

As it always was.

Freedom!

RELEASE

There's an expression I've heard: "Let it go… like a balloon… let it go!"

There's another expression that if you love something you should release them, and if they return they love you too.

There's another expression that if you give up family and friends that many more will be added to you.

I've had to release many things. I can't even count. Some have returned. Some have not. Some have been added. Some will not.

But I released everything.

It is so difficult to let things go. It is difficult to let friends go. Your loved ones. Your pet. Your job. Your house. Your church. Your religion. Your faith. Your gods. So many things. It is difficult to let things go.

But I discovered there are more difficult things to let go. Anger. Fear. Resentments. Griefs. Disappointments. Goals. Desire.

I am letting something go. It is important.
You've caught me here releasing my hurts.
My pain.
My sufferings.

I'm not denying them. I am, somehow, grateful for them. But I will not allow them to define me or determine me any longer. I've gone through so much. I have suffered so many things. For so long I allowed my pain and my hurts to tell me who I am. For so long I allowed myself to wear the tortured soul persona. Constantly wrestling!

No longer.

I am better for my sufferings,
but I am better than my sufferings.

Like this balloon, I am releasing my suffering. I am releasing my pain. I am releasing my disappointments. I am releasing my hurt. They have helped shape me. But their purpose has been served. They may be discarded. I release them.

Thank you. You may go!

I bear my wounds.
I bear them well.
I bear myself well.

RISING

Sophia has a significant relationship with the moon.
It is not direct light.
It is reflected light.

Leaving and even rejecting things that boasted direct light has meant that I have had to find my own light, discern new light from new sources in new places.

I have gained a new appreciation for the moon because it doesn't claim to be direct light. It humbly reflects it. But it is not light itself and never claims to be. I have a new appreciation for what it means to humbly acknowledge this.

I journey through darkness. The darkness of night. Because it is safer for me. It is like the dark night of the soul. I'll take whatever light is provided. And the moon does just fine for me right now.

I feel myself emerging,
being lifted up up up.
Even soaring.
Buoyant.
Life used to press me down.
Now I rise to it.

My freedom, my humble light… this is my food.

What freedom I now enjoy!
Nothing can stop me.
It used to be that everything and everyone
held me back and held me down.
I was constantly pressed and oppressed
by so many things
and so many ideas
and so many people.

Because I let them! I conspired.

It has taken some time to grow into this,
but now I know that I am no one's slave.
I am my own master.
I am liberated.
I will rise!

METAMPORPHOSIS

I visited a butterfly house.
It symbolizes in such beauty the intricacy
and delicacy of change.

My mind was filled with the urgency of change. The wonder of transformation. The beauty of a new creatio
The magnificence of metamorphosis.

There were some caterpillars and chrysalides hanging in a special chamber. How do those turn into these? From these crawling or dead-looking things to these free-flying beautiful creatures.

I look for this same thing in my own life. I know I am offensive to many. But I'm tired of gluing fake wings on an old shell. It's time for new life! True life!

The beauty of a butterfly's wings is most shown when their wings are open… in flight. They encouraged me to be more open, more honest. To fly and show my true colors.

Change is so difficult. Impossible! It is like a dying and rising. It's not like you can orchestrate it yourself. You can position yourself for change. Because when it comes to dying to self, who is it that puts you to death? Yo can't, because the you that would put you to death is still you.

There is an inexplicable power that does the final deed. Like resurrection, you wake up on the other side of transformation. You will never forget it because your life is changed forever. You are not the same person. But at the same time you are.

This is metamorphosis.

Out of sheer necessity Sophia has drummed up the courage to be transformed. And she is. She is changing. It is amazing to watch. And beautiful.

My journey requires considerable change in me. Actually, it has been a painful revelation of the transformatio that is urgent and necessary.

How does a caterpillar decide to become a butterfly?
I know metamorphosis is urgent. So I await.
I posture myself for transformation.
As I become more grounded, the change I need will come.
And, like the wings of a butterfly,
a light shines through me, and through you, to inspire others
to position themselves for change.

ANGEL

I didn't even know how I felt, I was so numb. My environment had become so toxic that I could no longer feel my emotions or see myself clearly. So I left everything and entered the world. I met people who though was amazing, cool, talented, fun and beautiful. Even perfect!

I am embarrassed for writing that previous paragraph. It reflects my first reaction to my new friends' opinion of me, which was embarrassment. I felt shame. Maybe they didn't know me well enough yet. In a matter of time they'll see me for who I really am and lose their positive opinion of me. But they didn't. They still loved me and thought I was amazing.

It reminded me of something Marianne Williamson wrote in **A Return to Love** that has spoken to this angel inside of me:

"Our deepest fear is not that we are inadequate. Our deepest fear is that we are powerful beyond measure. It is our light not our darkness that most frightens us. We ask ourselves, 'Who am I to be brilliant, gorgeous, talented and fabulous?' Actually, who are you not to be? You are a child of God. Your playing small does not serve the world. There is nothing enlightened about shrinking so that other people won't feel insecure aroun you. We are born to make manifest the glory of God that is within us. It is not just in some of us. It is in everyone. And as we let our light shine, we give other people permission to do the same. As we are liberated from our own fear, our presence automatically liberates others."

This image of Sophia is my favorite picture of my truest self. It captures me best. When I drew it, it conjured up all those memories. She is embarrassed. She feels ashamed. For her entire life she's been taught she is an unworthy, sinful worm. Nothing. Less than nothing. She was constantly kept in her place and criticized, and this toxin seeped through her self-love and poisoned her own vision of herself. She felt miserable about herself, a contamination in the world.

She mistook that for humility.
And then mistook that for virtue.

I finally escaped that toxic environment and am moving into the revelation of my own perfection. Even my own divinity! I am perfect just as I am. Deep down I know it's true, and soon I'll live as though it is.

Sophia is an angel.
She sees that now.
She knows that now.

And she likes it.

So do I.

LIGHT

Just before my escape I dreamed about a waterfall.
I saw that all things are One.
I knew the unity of all things.
This totally transformed my brain.

An immediate and lasting peace came to my mind, and all my theological, philosophical, intellectual, existential, and spiritual anxiety came to an abrupt end.

It died.
I came alive.
Everything changed.

This launched a series of external traumas in my life, including my escape.
I left everything and lost a lot.
I experienced a series of deprivations and a series of agonies.

When I was in captivity everything was tame.
After I escaped I became unfettered. Wild.
People noticed. I paid for it.

Sophia, drawn as a young woman, is our struggle from bondage to liberation.
It's me being courageous and independent.
It's my journey out of the confines and into unlimited freedom.

I spend a lot of time thinking about what has happened to me.
I realized the importance of my inner revolution. It was time to order my life accordingly. My inner truth demanded demonstration.

Curiously, I suddenly lost all inspiration to draw Sophia. I've concluded: Sophia has finished her journey, as I have finished mine. It's almost like she showed up to guide me. Thanks to Sophia, wisdom, I've come to a place. A good place.

So this image "Light" is a sign that she is… I am… I have… entered the Light.
I am in the Light. Completely. And it is so bright that you can't see her. Me. Individually. Distinctly. All is One We blur into each other. I am in the Light so much so that I can't be distinguished from it. Same for you. I an light. You are light.

Thanks for loving Sophia and her journey. Me and mine. You and yours.
Enjoy your freedom.

It is finished.

CONCLUSION

ly own personal Sophia journey was all about the deconstruction of my religion. It was launched by leaving e ministry and the church and all that entailed.

made the decision to leave because I felt trapped. It wasn't that I was no longer committed. I know the fference between being committed and being enslaved. I had been committed for over thirty years. But I as no longer committed when I came to the momentous realization that I had turned into a slave with a ctim mentality. Even though the church was an accomplice in this dynamic, I take full responsibility.

was just time for me to leave.
Ve mutually agreed.

ve been accused of being a false shepherd because I abandoned the sheep. I don't see it that way. Rather, I e myself as the shepherd who left the ninety-nine to search for the one.

irst I found myself.
Now I find others who are like me.

have no idea what your story is. Perhaps you feel trapped in a relationship, a job, a school, a life… I don't now. In any case, it doesn't feel like commitment anymore. It feels like slavery. It feels like bondage. It feels ke being trapped.

hope this story about Sophia inspires you. I hope she helps you find the courage you already have to make our move.

t won't be easy. Finding your own independence, fighting for it and then keeping it, never is easy.

But it is always worth it.

May your own Sophia guide you.

Peace on your path!

Made in the USA
Monee, IL
03 August 2020

37496521R10081